LSAT®
PrepTest 75
Unlocked

Exclusive Data, Analysis & Explanations for the June 2015 LSAT

KAPLAN

PUBLISHING

New York

© 2017 by Kaplan, Inc.

Published by Kaplan Publishing, a division of Kaplan, Inc.
750 Third Avenue
New York, NY 10017

ISBN: 978-1-5062-2332-2
10 9 8 7 6 5 4 3 2 1

The Inside Story

PrepTest 75 was administered in June 2015. It challenged 23,238 test takers. What made this test so hard? Here's a breakdown of what Kaplan students who were surveyed after taking the official exam considered PrepTest 75's most difficult section.

Hardest PrepTest 75 Section as Reported by Test Takers

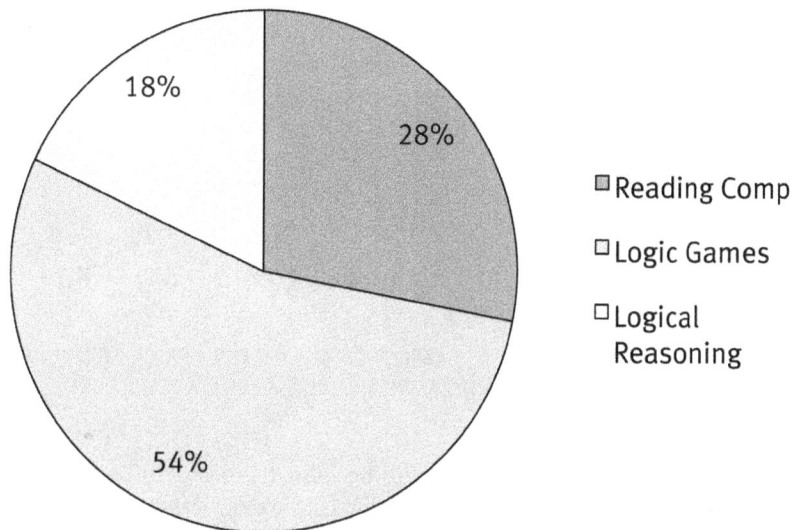

18%

28%

54%

▣ Reading Comp

▢ Logic Games

▢ Logical
   Reasoning

Based on these results, you might think that studying Logic Games is the key to LSAT success. Well, Logic Games is important, but test takers' perceptions don't tell the whole story. For that, you need to consider students' actual performance. The following chart shows the average number of students to miss each question in each of PrepTest 75's different sections.

Percentage Incorrect by PrepTest 75 Section Type

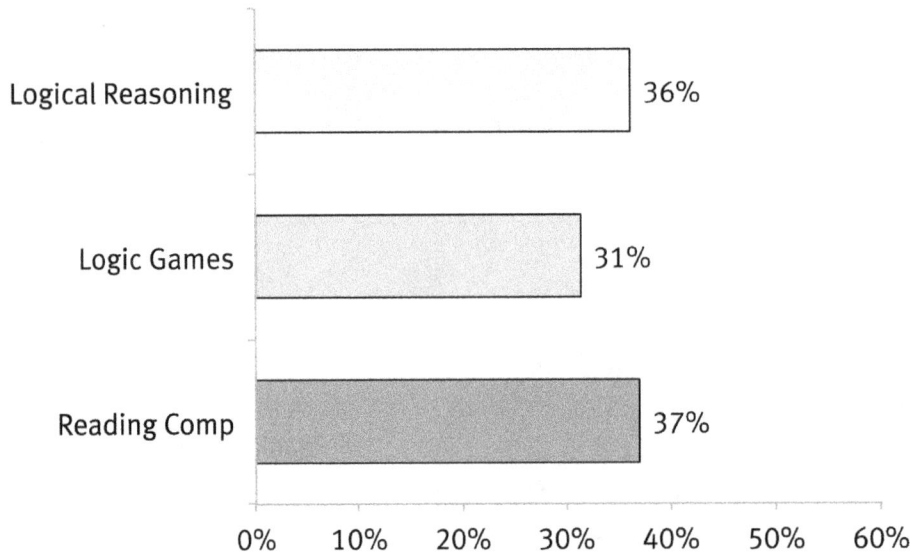

Section	Percentage
Logical Reasoning	36%
Logic Games	31%
Reading Comp	37%

(Scale: 0% 10% 20% 30% 40% 50% 60%)

Actual student performance tells quite a different story. On average, students were almost equally likely to miss questions in all three of the different section types, and on PrepTest 75, Reading Comprehension and Logical Reasoning were somewhat higher than Logic Games in actual difficulty.

Maybe students overestimate the difficulty of the Logic Games section because it's so unusual, or maybe it's because a really hard Logic Game is so easy to remember after the test. But the truth is that the test maker places hard questions throughout the test. Here were the locations of the 10 hardest (most missed) questions in the exam.

Location of 10 Most Difficult Questions in PrepTest 75

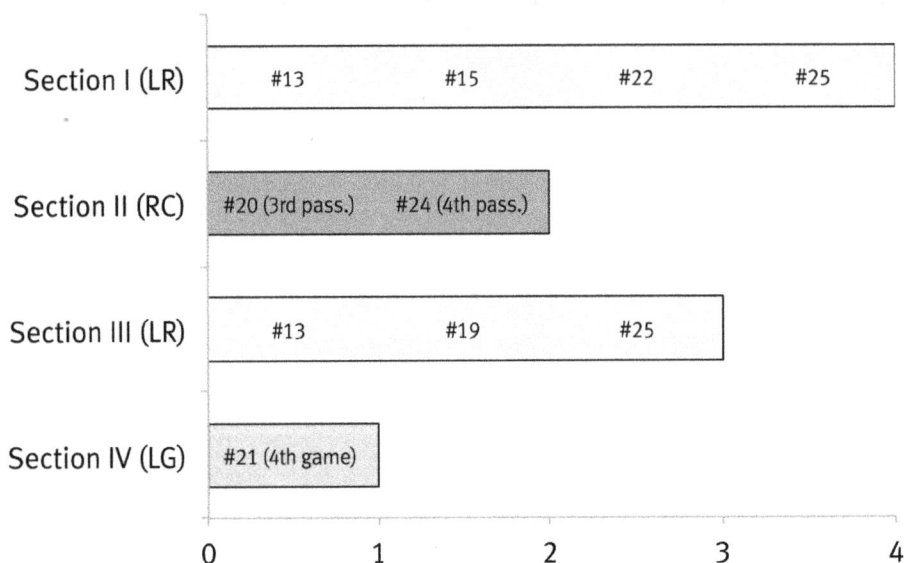

Section	Questions
Section I (LR)	#13 #15 #22 #25
Section II (RC)	#20 (3rd pass.) #24 (4th pass.)
Section III (LR)	#13 #19 #25
Section IV (LG)	#21 (4th game)

(Scale: 0 1 2 3 4)

KAPLAN

The takeaway from this data is that, to maximize your potential on the LSAT, you need to take a comprehensive approach. Test yourself rigorously, and review your performance on every section of the test. Kaplan's LSAT explanations provide the expertise and insight you need to fully understand your results. The explanations are written and edited by a team of LSAT experts, who have helped thousands of students improve their scores. Kaplan always provides data-driven analysis of the test, ranking the difficulty of every question based on actual student performance. The ten hardest questions on every test are highlighted with a 4-star difficulty rating, the highest we give. The analysis breaks down the remaining questions into 1-, 2-, and 3-star ratings so that you can compare your performance to thousands of other test takers on all LSAC material.

Don't settle for wondering whether a question was really as hard as it seemed to you. Analyze the test with real data, and learn the secrets and strategies that help top scorers master the LSAT.

7 Can't–Miss Features of PrepTest 75

- This was the first PrepTest numbered in the "70s" with 100, rather than 101 questions.
- PrepTest 75 marked the first time since September 2007 (PT 53) that an LSAT was administered without any Strict Sequencing games, and it was only the third released LSAT ever to have two Distribution games.
- The fourth and final game on PrepTest 75—Business Newsletter—has an extremely rare feature: one entity that occupies two spaces. (Even the LSAT experts were talking about that one.)
- In Logical Reasoning, PrepTest 75 was the third consecutive LSAT with no Point at Issue questions.
- PrepTest 75 was the only test released in 2014–2015 in which no Reading Comprehension passage had eight questions.
- Test takers who made good predictions in Reading Comprehension saved a lot of time reading through answers. Only 7 of the 27 answers in RC were (D) or (E).
- The #1 song in the country when PrepTest 75 was released was Wiz Khalifa's "See You Again" from the *Furious 7* soundtrack. LSAT students know you need to be fast *and* furious on this test.

PrepTest 75 in Context

As much fun as it is to find out what makes a PrepTest unique or noteworthy, it's even more important to know just how representative it is of other LSAT administrations (and, thus, how likely it is to be representative of the exam you will face on Test Day). The following charts compare the numbers of each kind of question and game on PrepTest 75 to the average numbers seen on all officially released LSATs administered over the past five years (from 2012 through 2016).

Number of LR Questions by Type: PrepTest 75 vs. 2012–2016 Average

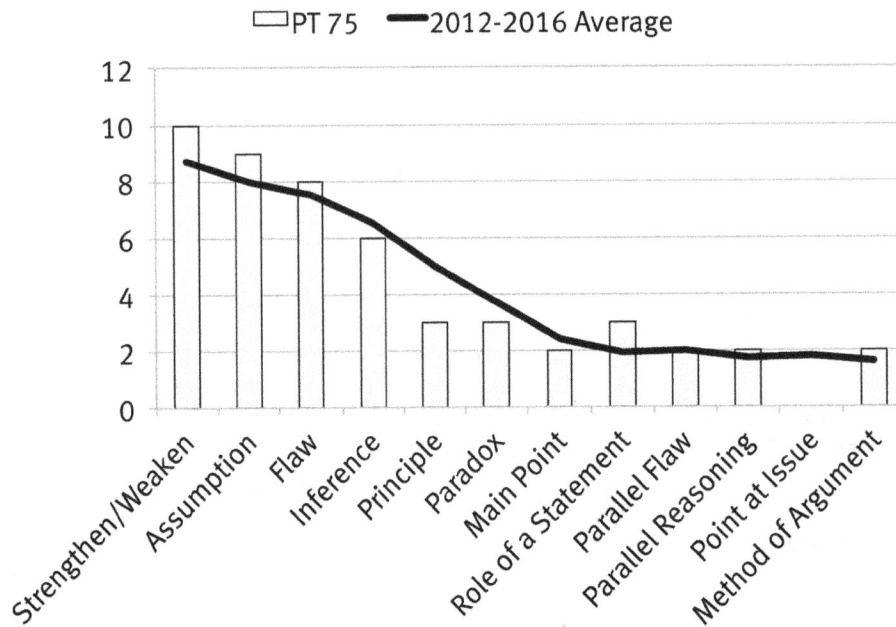

Number of LG Games by Type: PrepTest 75 vs. 2012–2016 Average

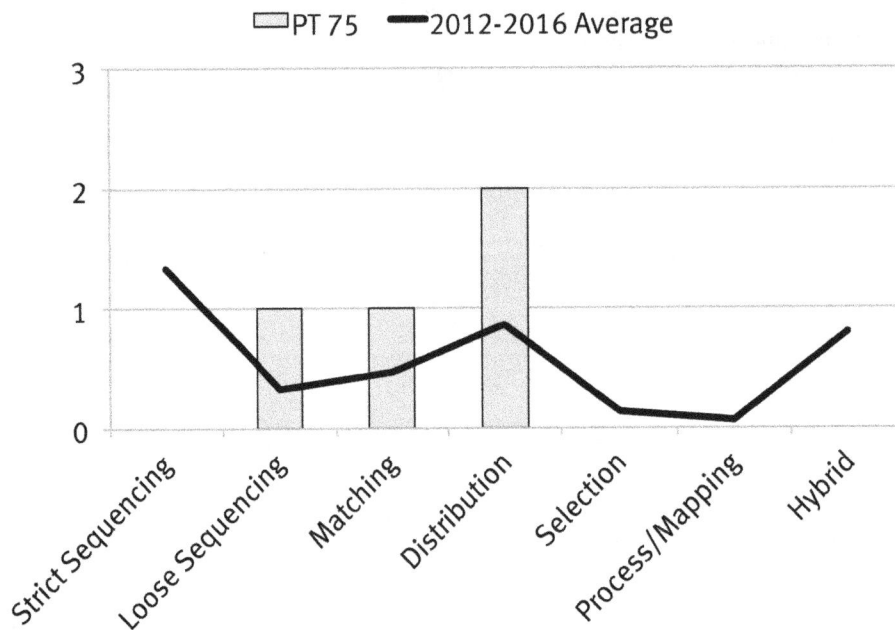

Number of RC Questions by Type: PrepTest 75 vs. 2012–2016 Average

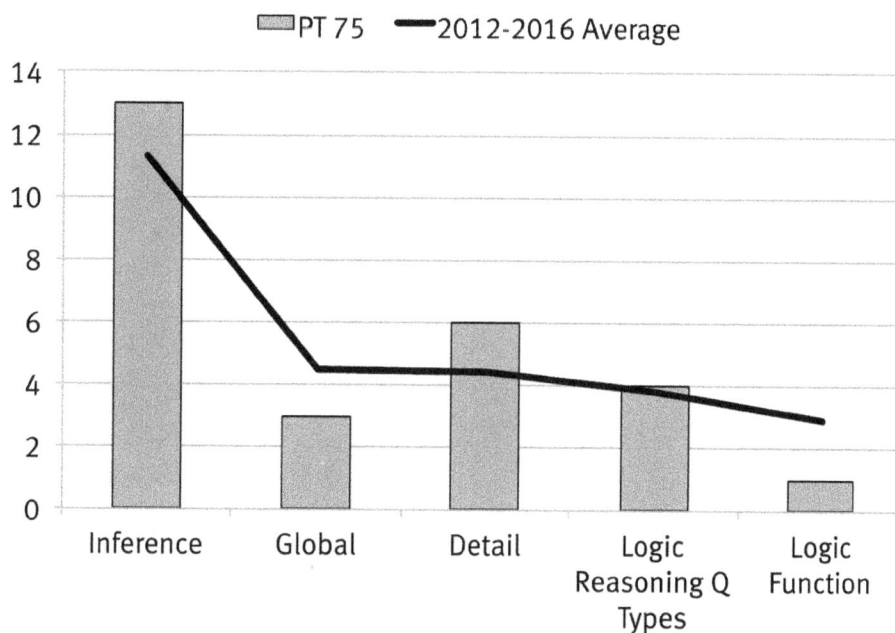

There isn't usually a huge difference in the distribution of questions from LSAT to LSAT, but if this test seems harder (or easier) to you than another you've taken, compare the number of questions of the types on which you, personally, are strongest and weakest. And then, explore within each section to see if your best or worst question types came earlier or later.

Students in Kaplan's comprehensive LSAT courses have access to every released LSAT, and to an online Q-Bank with thousands of officially released questions, games, and passages. If you are studying on your own, you have to do a bit more work to identify your strengths and your areas of opportunity. Quantitative analysis (like that in the charts above) is an important tool for understanding how the test is constructed, and how you are performing on it.

Section I: Logical Reasoning

Q#	Question Type	Correct	Difficulty
1	Assumption (Necessary)	B	★
2	Principle (Identify/Strengthen)	C	★
3	Assumption (Necessary)	A	★
4	Method of Argument	E	★★
5	Weaken	C	★
6	Paradox	D	★★
7	Flaw	E	★
8	Main Point	C	★
9	Strengthen	A	★
10	Principle (Identify/Strengthen)	E	★
11	Weaken	D	★★
12	Flaw	D	★★
13	Inference	C	★★★★
14	Role of a Statement	A	★
15	Strengthen	C	★★★★
16	Role of a Statement	C	★
17	Inference	D	★★★
18	Flaw	B	★★
19	Paradox	B	★
20	Inference	E	★★
21	Strengthen	B	★★★
22	Parallel Flaw	C	★★★★
23	Assumption (Sufficient)	C	★★★
24	Flaw	E	★★★
25	Parallel Reasoning	A	★★★★

KAPLAN

1. (B) Assumption (Necessary)

Step 1: Identify the Question Type

This is a Necessary Assumption question because it asks for the assumption that the argument *requires*.

Step 2: Untangle the Stimulus

The pundit concludes that the city erred when it sold the right to assess parking fees to a private company. The evidence is that the private company has made huge profits from raising parking fees—profits that the pundit says could have gone to the city.

Step 3: Make a Prediction

In order for the pundit's conclusion to be valid, one has to assume that the city had the same capacity as the private company to raise parking fees.

Step 4: Evaluate the Answer Choices

(B) matches this prediction perfectly. Remember that on Necessary Assumption questions, the Denial Test is a great way to double-check your answer or to evaluate an answer choice if prediction is tough. In this case, to deny **(B)** would be to say that the city *could not* have raised parking fees had it not sold away the rights. If that's the case, the city would never have seen that extra money, and the pundit's argument is in jeopardy.

(A) is Outside the Scope. The pundit is concerned with whether or not the city made a mistake to sell the rights at all, not with how many companies were willing to pay for those rights.

(C) is Extreme. It broadens the issue to say *all* municipal functions "should always" be handled by the municipality. However, the pundit's argument focuses specifically on one function, so **(C)** doesn't have to be true for the argument to work.

(D) is not necessary for the argument to be valid. Using the Denial Test, even if the revenue from parking fees *is* the only factor to consider when setting rates, the pundit can still argue that it was a mistake for the city to privatize parking fee collection. After all, in the pundit's case, the only consideration was about how much revenue the private companies have been able to raise.

(E) is Outside the Scope. The relative efficiency of private companies versus city officials when it comes to parking fees is not at issue.

2. (C) Principle (Identify/Strengthen)

Step 1: Identify the Question Type

The phrase "[w]hich one of the following principles" identifies this as an Identify the Principle question. Furthermore,

"justify the reasoning" indicates that the correct answer will be a broadly stated principle that strengthens the argument.

Step 2: Untangle the Stimulus

The argument's conclusion is signaled by *therefore*: popular science publications should stop trying to reach a wide audience with their explanations of new scientific developments. The evidence describes a dilemma: when these publications try to reach wide audiences, they skimp on scientific accuracy. When they aim for more scientific rigor, they succeed but lose their broad appeal.

Step 3: Make a Prediction

In order for its recommendation to be valid, the argument assumes that getting the science right is a more important goal to achieve than appealing to a broad swath of the public. The correct answer will be a general principle supporting this.

Step 4: Evaluate the Answer Choices

(C) is worded in the negative, but says the exact same thing as the prediction.

(A) could help publications reconcile the goal of reaching a wide audience with that of staying scientifically accurate, but the author recommends disregarding wide audiences altogether.

(B) doesn't affect the argument. The author argues against trying to reach wide audiences because doing so risks getting the science wrong, not because doing so is merely difficult. How recent the science is is not mentioned.

(D) is a 180 because it weakens the author's argument in favor of abandoning the goal of reaching a wide audience.

(E) misses the point of the argument. The excessive use of metaphor in science publications often muddies the science, but the author isn't arguing for or against the abandonment of metaphors entirely, so **(E)** doesn't strengthen the reasoning.

3. (A) Assumption (Necessary)

Step 1: Identify the Question Type

This is a Necessary Assumption question because it seeks an assumption "on which the critic's argument relies."

Step 2: Untangle the Stimulus

The critic bleakly concludes that rock music no longer has anything going for it. The evidence is that rock music has always been bad, both musically and socially, but at least back in the LP era, album covers featured distinctive visual art. Nowadays, though, the success of digital music has all but eliminated LPs.

Step 3: Make a Prediction

The critic assumes that innovative visual art disappeared along with the old LP covers. The correct answer will paraphrase this idea.

Step 4: Evaluate the Answer Choices

(A) is therefore correct. Applying the Denial Test, if digital music *is* actually distributed with accompanying innovative visual art, then rock music does still have at least one positive feature, and the critic's argument is impaired.

(B) is a 180. It goes against the argument by suggesting that rock LPs, which feature innovative visual art, are still being mass-produced.

(C) is Extreme. It doesn't have to be true that rock LPs were the only LPs to contain innovative album cover art. Even if other genres also had innovative art, the critic could still speak highly of those rock albums that had it, too.

(D) doesn't have to be true for the critic's argument to be valid. Even if today's LPs do not have innovative album cover art, the critic can still argue that rock music has nothing to recommend it these days.

(E) is an Irrelevant Comparison. The critic says that rock music is currently "musically bankrupt and socially destructive," so it doesn't need to be true that rock music was even worse in the past for the argument to work.

4. (E) Method of Argument

Step 1: Identify the Question Type

This is a Method of Argument question because it asks you to determine "how the ... argument proceeds."

Step 2: Untangle the Stimulus

The scientist concludes that babbling is a linguistic task. The evidence is a study in which researchers set out to determine whether babbling was a linguistic task or just random sounds. Their results were the opposite of those one would expect for nonlinguistic vocalizations, so babbling must therefore be a linguistic task.

Step 3: Make a Prediction

On Method of Argument questions, focus on what the argument *does*, not on the specifics of what it says. Here, the scientist establishes the argument's conclusion by presenting a scientific observation and then ruling out one of two competing explanations for the observation, thereby settling on the other explanation.

Step 4: Evaluate the Answer Choices

(E) is therefore correct.

(A) doesn't take into account any of the experimental evidence presented, and the scientist never makes any counterarguments in order to disprove anything.

(B) would be correct if the scientist said that researchers started out assuming that babbling was a nonlinguistic task, but no such principle was held as true by the researchers prior to their experiment.

(C) is a Distortion. The scientist does describe an experiment used to answer a question, but the point of the argument is not to establish that the experiment was *necessary* to answer the question. The scientist merely uses the experiment as evidence to draw a larger conclusion.

(D) is partially correct in that the scientist does present an explanation. However, the scientist never mentions anyone's assertions that the explanation is "unlikely to be correct," let alone counters them.

5. (C) Weaken

Step 1: Identify the Question Type

The phrase "weaken the ... argument" is a clear indication of a Weaken question.

Step 2: Untangle the Stimulus

The environment minister's conclusion is that planting lots of trees will help the country fulfill its commitment to reducing carbon dioxide emissions over the next decade. The evidence is that trees absorb carbon dioxide.

Step 3: Make a Prediction

In order for the environment minister's prediction to come true, planting trees would have to absorb more carbon dioxide than it releases. Otherwise, the relative amount of carbon dioxide in the atmosphere would increase. Therefore, the argument is weakened by anything suggesting that planting trees can actually increase carbon dioxide emissions.

Step 4: Evaluate the Answer Choices

(C), if true, weakens the argument by suggesting that planting trees could increase the overall amount of carbon dioxide.

(A) doesn't weaken the argument. Nothing in the minister's reasoning indicates that the government wouldn't be able to financially incentivize landowners to give up their land for tree planting. Alternatively, they could just plant the trees on public land.

(B) would affect the argument if you knew how much deforested land would need to be replanted with trees to absorb a given amount of carbon dioxide. Without this information though, **(B)** isn't a weakener.

(D) is Outside the Scope because the minister is specifically concerned with how the country can fulfill the commitment it has made, which is to reduce carbon dioxide emissions in the 10 years allotted. Whether different commitments would be better is immaterial.

(E) is Outside the Scope. The country has committed itself to combating global warming by decreasing its carbon dioxide output. Other gases are therefore irrelevant to the fulfillment of that commitment.

6. (D) Paradox

Step 1: Identify the Question Type

If a question stem asks for the answer choice that "most helps to account for" a given phenomenon or discrepancy, it's a Paradox question.

Step 2: Untangle the Stimulus

The stimulus describes a contradiction concerning SUV safety. In an accident, SUVs, though expensive, are safer for their occupants than are smaller vehicles. However, auto safety experts still conclude that the rising popularity of SUVs is cause for concern.

Step 3: Make a Prediction

You don't have to have a hard-and-fast prediction for Paradox questions. But you do need to know how to spot the correct answer when you come to it. In this case, the correct answer will explain why auto safety experts are still alarmed despite the popularity of vehicles that are relatively safer.

Step 4: Evaluate the Answer Choices

(D) explains the discrepancy by suggesting that SUV-involved collisions produce more fatalities generally. In other words, the SUV occupants are safer, but it's now the people in the smaller vehicles that are in more danger.

(A) is a 180. It deepens the paradox because it suggests that SUV owners will drive more carefully, which should relieve auto safety experts, not unnerve them.

(B) is Outside the Scope. It introduces the idea of fuel consumption, which doesn't come up at all in the stimulus.

(C) doesn't explain the paradox because it suggests that more people will be riding in safer vehicles. If that's the case, why the alarm? Unless an increase in passenger numbers indicates an increase in danger, this choice doesn't explain the safety experts' alarm.

(E) doesn't account for the experts' concern because, on balance, SUVs are safer cars, so knowing that they are equally as likely as smaller vehicles to be involved in collisions shouldn't necessarily cause alarm.

7. (E) Flaw

Step 1: Identify the Question Type

This is a Flaw question because it asks how the argument is "vulnerable to criticism." Find the conclusion, evidence, and assumption, then note the disconnect in the reasoning.

Step 2: Untangle the Stimulus

The political advertisement is firmly against Sherwood's bid for reelection to city council. Sherwood apparently campaigns against higher taxes, but while Sherwood was on the city council, the council voted to raise taxes. Therefore, the argument says, Sherwood should be defeated at the polls.

Step 3: Make a Prediction

This argument commits the classic fallacy of division, which is just a fancy way of saying that it imputes a characteristic of a whole to each of its constituent parts. In this case, it can certainly be true that Sherwood voted against higher taxes but was just outvoted by her colleagues.

Step 4: Evaluate the Answer Choices

(E) accurately states the advertisement's logical flaw.

(A) is almost a 180. The political advertisement draws a conclusion about a specific person based on a more general assertion about a collective to which that person belongs. Conversely, **(A)** suggests that argument makes a broader generalization on a specific instance.

(B) would be relevant if the advertisement suggested that higher taxes were somehow unavoidable. But whether or not higher taxes can be avoided doesn't figure into the argument.

(C) describes the common Formal Logic flaw of necessity versus sufficiency. However, no Formal Logic is involved in this argument.

(D) describes an ad hominem attack, but the advertisement doesn't target Sherwood's character. Rather, the advertisement assumes that Sherwood must have taken the same actions taken by the city council as a whole.

8. (C) Main Point

Step 1: Identify the Question Type

Any question stem asking you to find the "main conclusion" of an argument is a Main Point question.

Step 2: Untangle the Stimulus

On a Main Point question, the entire task is to determine an argument's conclusion. Therefore, you're unlikely to find those helpful Keywords that point directly to conclusions in the stimuli for other question types. Instead, look for a strong statement of the author's point of view and use the One-Sentence Test to find the single sentence the client would insist on in making that point.

Step 3: Make a Prediction

The client's point of view comes in the third sentence. The catering company has decided to raise its rates, arguing that their expanding client base has necessitated hiring new staff. But the client concludes that the catering company should reconsider. The last sentence is support for the conclusion:

raising rates, in the client's view, would compromise the company's mission to provide low-cost catering.

Step 4: Evaluate the Answer Choices

(C) is a match for this prediction.

(A) restates the first sentence of the argument, but this is merely background information on which the client bases the argument.

(B) is a 180. The client clearly argues that the catering company should *not* raise its rates.

(D) is evidence that the client uses to support the claim that the company shouldn't increase its rates.

(E), like **(D)**, is support for the client's conclusion, and not the conclusion itself.

9. (A) Strengthen

Step 1: Identify the Question Type

The phrase "strengthens the support for the … hypothesis" indicates a Strengthen question.

Step 2: Untangle the Stimulus

The scientists hypothesize that the erratic flight style of the red admiral butterfly evolved to help them avoid predators. Their evidence is that because the red admiral is not poisonous, it needed to evolve other means of avoiding predators in order to survive.

Step 3: Make a Prediction

In order for the scientists to reach their hypothesis, they assume that the red admiral's flight style didn't evolve for any other reason than to avoid predators. They further assume that poisonous species of butterfly don't also have the same irregular flight style. The correct answer will validate either of these assumptions.

Step 4: Evaluate the Answer Choices

(A), if true, strengthens the argument by suggesting that poisonous butterflies, which predators already avoid, don't need an irregular flight style. It's therefore more likely that the flight style developed to help avoid predators. **(A)** doesn't prove the conclusion, but it does make it more likely.

(B) doesn't affect the argument because other causes of death for butterflies are Outside the Scope.

(C) doesn't strengthen the argument unless you know that those other species with the same flight pattern have developed those flight patterns to avoid predators. Simply knowing that other species have the same flight style as the red admiral doesn't explain why that style evolved.

(D) is an Irrelevant Comparison. How other varieties of insects behave doesn't matter unless it helps indicate whether the irregular flight pattern evolved as a means to avoid predators. **(D)** may even weaken the argument if it is suggesting that the

red admiral's flight style evolved to conserve energy rather than to help them avoid predators.

(E) is Outside the Scope because the scientists don't assume that the red admiral's predators feed exclusively on the red admiral.

10. (E) Principle (Identify/Strengthen)

Step 1: Identify the Question Type

This is an Identify the Principle question in which the correct answer will be a broadly stated rule that "supports the reasoning," or strengthens the argument.

Step 2: Untangle the Stimulus

The author argues that copyright statutes grant copyright protections for too long a period of time. The support for this conclusion is that the cost to society of granting additional years of copyright (the creation of protected monopolies) exceeds the benefit (the incentive to produce original works).

Step 3: Make a Prediction

To strengthen this argument, the argument assumes that society should adopt statutes that produce societal benefits larger than their societal costs. The correct answer will be a broad principle that restates this idea.

Step 4: Evaluate the Answer Choices

(E) is therefore correct.

(A) is Outside the Scope because the argument concerns the effects of copyright statutes, not their aims. Furthermore, the statutes as written do not have *inconsistent* aims. They are set up to benefit society and encourage people to create original works. The author just thinks they provide too much benefit, as written, and thus have the unintended consequence of having a societal cost.

(B) doesn't strengthen the argument because the author never points to any changing conditions that impact whether or not copyright statutes are still justified.

(C) is Outside the Scope of the argument. The author doesn't argue for expanding copyright statutes to all countries; rather, the author argues that those countries that have adopted such statutes grant protections for too long a period.

(D) is also Outside the Scope. The author relies on a societal cost-benefit analysis to support the reasoning; the argument doesn't trade on whether or not copyright laws limit or enhance individual *rights*.

11. (D) Weaken

Step 1: Identify the Question Type

The phrase "calls into question" indicates a Weaken question.

Step 2: Untangle the Stimulus

The police chief concludes that his policing strategy has decreased crime in the city by 20 percent. The strategy boasts real-time crime data and an allocation of resources to the areas with the highest crime rates.

Step 3: Make a Prediction

Causal arguments such as this one are very common in Logical Reasoning, particularly in Strengthen and Weaken questions. Here, the chief notices an effect (the decline in the city's crime rate) and argues for a cause (the chief's own policing strategy). To weaken a causal argument, find an answer choice that suggests an alternative cause.

Step 4: Evaluate the Answer Choices

(D) provides that alternative cause by associating the city's decreasing crime rate with an overall decline in crime nationwide. The police chief surely didn't implement the strategy throughout the whole country, so the strategy may not be responsible for the city's lower crime rate.

(A) is an Irrelevant Comparison. Even if the city's crime rate is still relatively high, it can still be lower than it once was thanks to the chief's strategy.

(B) is also an Irrelevant Comparison because the argument is restricted to the chief's own tenure and the rates immediately before the chief started. It doesn't incorporate any other periods—certainly not from decades earlier.

(C) is not a valid weakener because it's not relevant to the argument to know when exactly during the chief's tenure the crime rate decreased. Perhaps the strategy was implemented quickly and successfully, and that's why it has since leveled off. In that case, **(C)** could be seen as a strengthener.

(E) is an Irrelevant Comparison because the chief is making an argument about the city as a whole. The relative crime rates of different parts of that city don't figure into the argument.

12. (D) Flaw

Step 1: Identify the Question Type

Because the question stem indicates that the commentator's argument is already "vulnerable to criticism," this is a Flaw question.

Step 2: Untangle the Stimulus

The commentator concludes that the Duke of Acredia was correct in asserting that concern for the people's welfare is necessary for good governance.

If	*successful governance*	→	*concern for the welfare of the people*

The evidence is that the fall of Acredian governments *always* coincided with the rule of leaders who disregarded the people's welfare.

If	*~ successful governance*	→	*~ concern for the welfare of the people*

Step 3: Make a Prediction

The word *necessary* in the argument's conclusion may have tipped you off to the flaw that the commentator commits. In his conclusion, the commentator makes the mistake of negating without reversing. The evidence says that when governments have fallen, the rulers have *always* "viciously disregarded the people's needs." The commentator mistakes a sufficient condition with a necessary one.

Step 4: Evaluate the Answer Choices

(D) accurately describes this flaw.

(A) is a Distortion. The argument doesn't concern the conditions necessary for the welfare of the people; the argument concerns one condition the commentator claims is necessary for successful governance of the people.

(B) comes close, but goes wrong when it alleges that the commentator's inference is based on the fact that the absence of concern for the people's welfare has always *led to* failure. The evidence doesn't describe causation. Instead, the evidence says "when … governments have fallen," their falls have always been when rulers were not concerned with the people. So, the evidence *does* set up Formal Logic, but not in the order of a causal relationship in which the lack of care *caused* the government's failure.

(C) is not the argument's flaw because the commentator gives no information about the sources used to gather the argument's evidence.

(E) is incorrect because the commentator isn't doing anything nearly as broad as assessing the character of past leaders. Moreover, even if the argument were to assess these leaders' character with words such as *concerned* or *vicious*, it doesn't pretend to do so using an objective standard.

13. (C) Inference

Step 1: Identify the Question Type

This is an Inference question because it asks for the answer choice "most supported by [the] statements."

Step 2: Untangle the Stimulus

Dr. Khan starts by sharing a discrepancy: recent observations of the solar system don't confirm earlier ones, which showed the presence of a comet reservoir. Professor Burns infers from this discrepancy that the earlier observations must therefore be incorrect. However, the recent observations happened under poor conditions.

Step 3: Make a Prediction

Determine what must be true from Dr. Khan's statements. If the recent observations occurred under poor conditions, then any conclusions based on those observations would be called into question. Therefore, Professor Burns may be rash in tossing out the earlier observations based solely on newer ones that could be untrustworthy.

Step 4: Evaluate the Answer Choices

(C) is therefore a valid inference.

(A) can't be inferred. It doesn't have to be true that the recent observations would have definitely confirmed the earlier ones had they been carried out under better conditions.

(B) is a Distortion. The recent observations don't have to confirm the earlier ones; Dr. Khan is simply implying that Professor Burns is wrong to claim that the recent observations invalidate the earlier ones.

(D) isn't a valid inference. For all we know, Dr. Khan may believe that the recent observations, if made under better conditions, *would* be enough to invalidate the earlier ones. But since the recent observations were made under poor conditions, we'll never know.

(E) is Extreme. Dr. Khan doesn't imply that the recent observations are *worthless*. The poor conditions under which the recent observations were made are not sufficient to throw out the earlier observations, but that doesn't mean the recent observations might not have some other value.

14. (A) Role of a Statement

Step 1: Identify the Question Type

This is a Role of a Statement question because it asks you to determine the "role played in the argument" by a particular claim.

Step 2: Untangle the Stimulus

The author begins by conceding a point: society would improve if people avoided impoliteness. The word [b]ut beginning the second sentence signals the author's point of view: despite the earlier point, society would not be served by laws mandating politeness. The last sentence provides support: enforcing those laws would create more problems than would impoliteness.

Step 3: Make a Prediction

The sentence in question is the author's main point, or conclusion. The first sentence provides background, and the last sentence is evidence.

Step 4: Evaluate the Answer Choices

(A) is therefore correct.

(B) is a 180. It's the last sentence that serves as evidence to support the author's conclusion.

(C) is two steps removed. The claim in question is the author's main point, one that the rest of the argument is designed to support.

(D) is incorrect because the statement in question is itself the main conclusion. It is neither a premise of the argument, nor an illustration of such. In fact, the whole argument speaks in generalizations; there are no specific illustrations.

(E) is incorrect because the author never describes a phenomenon in the argument. Rather, each sentence of the argument describes a hypothetical situation. (E) also indicates the claim in question is not the conclusion, when in fact it is.

15. (C) Strengthen

Step 1: Identify the Question Type

The phrase "strengthen the … argument" is a clear indication of a Strengthen question.

Step 2: Untangle the Stimulus

Don't be thrown by the scientific subject matter. This argument, like many others, attempts to explain a phenomenon. In this case, the phenomenon is the oval orbits of most planets that revolve around distant stars. This is contrasted with planets in our solar system, several of which have circular orbits. However, the astronomer notes that comets with oval orbits in our solar system got those orbits through encounters with planets within the same solar system. Therefore, says the astronomer, those distant planets probably acquired their oval orbits in the same way.

Step 3: Make a Prediction

The astronomer assumes that just because at least some comets in our solar system with oval orbits acquired those orbits through encounters with other objects, the same must be true of planets with oval orbits around distant stars. In other words, the author assumes that the same conditions causing the oval orbits of comets are present for planets orbiting distant stars. The correct answer will validate this assumption.

Step 4: Evaluate the Answer Choices

(C) strengthens the argument by indicating that there are indeed other planets that the planets in oval orbits could have encountered. (C) doesn't prove that the astronomer is correct, but it makes the conclusion more likely to be true.

(A) references the relative size of planets, which doesn't figure into the argument. You don't know from the argument whether the planets thrown into oval orbits are usually the smaller ones. Knowing which object would adjust its orbit doesn't make it any more likely that the oval orbits of distant planets were actually caused by close encounters with other planets.

(B) doesn't affect the astronomer's argument, which is concerned with whether encounters with other planets render a planet's orbit oval in shape. Even if some of the planets orbiting our sun do have oval orbits, there's no information in **(B)** indicating what caused those oval orbits, so **(B)** can't be a strengthener.

(D) helps to confirm a piece of the astronomer's evidence—that comets *can* change to oval orbits based on close encounters with other objects—but it doesn't help validate the conclusion the astronomer draws about the planets orbiting distant stars.

(E) is a 180. It weakens the argument by suggesting that no other objects could have affected the orbit of planets surrounding a distant star, even though we know most of those distant planets have an oval orbit.

16. (C) Role of a Statement

Step 1: Identify the Question Type

A question stem asking you to determine the "role played in the argument" by any claim is a Role of a Statement question.

Step 2: Untangle the Stimulus

The argument's conclusion comes in the second sentence: irrigating crops with seawater would be cheaper than most other irrigated agriculture if the crops were grown near oceans. The evidence is threefold: The water used in such irrigation would not have to be pumped far. The greatest expense in irrigated agriculture comes from pumping the water, and such expenses increase with the distance the water is pumped.

Step 3: Make a Prediction

The claim in question, that the greatest expense in irrigated agriculture is in pumping the water, is given in support of the conclusion that irrigating crops with seawater is cheaper if the crops are grown near oceans. Simply put, the claim is one of the pieces of evidence.

Step 4: Evaluate the Answer Choices

(C) is therefore correct.

(A) is incorrect because there are no claims in the argument that the author disproves.

(B) is a 180. Not only is the statement question not held out as a hypothesis, but it supports the argument's conclusion rather than undermining it.

(D) is incorrect because the argument's conclusion is the conditional prediction in the second sentence. The claim in question is a fact supporting that prediction.

(E) describes a subsidiary conclusion. **(E)** is correct in that the claim in question is not the argument's conclusion. However, the argument provides no evidence to support the idea that pumping water is the greatest expense in irrigated agriculture.

17. (D) Inference

Step 1: Identify the Question Type

This is an Inference question because it asks you to accept the stimulus (the "statements above") as true, and then determine which answer choice they "most strongly support."

Step 2: Untangle the Stimulus

The stimulus outlines a worry of critics: gloomy news about the economy decreases public confidence in the economy, of which everyone has direct daily experience. Journalists can't be concerned, though, with the effects of their work if they're to do that work well. Further, people don't turn to journalists unless it's on a matter of which they have no direct experience.

Step 3: Make a Prediction

On Inference questions, try to link statements together to see if a prediction emerges naturally. People don't defer to journalists on matters they directly experience. Because everyone has direct daily experience with the economy, it must be true that people don't defer to journalists when it comes to reports on the economy.

Step 4: Evaluate the Answer Choices

(D) is a good paraphrase of this inference.

(A) is a Distortion. The critics may very well be right that people's confidence in the economy has an effect on it, but the stimulus is more concerned with the critics' worry about the effects of bleak news reports on the economy. Those news reports aren't affecting people's confidence, but their confidence may still be affecting the economy.

(B) is a Distortion. The stimulus suggests that people aren't terribly affected by bad news reports on matters of which they have direct experience, but that doesn't mean that the critics' worry carries over to matters like foreign policy, of which people don't have daily experience. In that case, the news reports *may* affect people's foreign policy views, but perhaps the impact of people's mood on foreign policy is not discernible.

(C) restates the critics' worry, but that doesn't mean that the worry must be valid. If anything, this is a 180 because the author's statements, taken together, indicate that the worry might be unfounded.

(E) paraphrases the journalists' view, but that doesn't mean that this view is valid. It could still be true that journalists *should* be concerned about the effects of their work; this stimulus is merely suggesting that those effects aren't significant when it comes to people's perceptions of the economy.

18. (B) Flaw

Step 1: Identify the Question Type

Any question stem asking you to determine why an argument is "vulnerable to criticism" is a Flaw question.

Step 2: Untangle the Stimulus

The police captain rejects recent claims that there's graft in her precinct. The evidence for this is that the chief of police has indicated that gifts over $100 in value qualify as graft, and no such gifts have exchanged hands within the precinct.

Step 3: Make a Prediction

This would be a solid argument as long as gifts over $100 in value are the *only* possible instances of graft. The police chief never indicated that, however; the captain merely assumed it. The definition of graft could be large enough to encompass many different actions, some of which may have occurred at the precinct in question.

Step 4: Evaluate the Answer Choices

(B) is a good paraphrase for this overlooked possibility.

(A) is not the flaw because there's no "limited sample." The police captain accounts for every single officer in the precinct, and the accusations of graft are focused only on that precinct.

(C) is Outside the Scope. The captain's rebuttal focuses only on certain actions that the officers in the precinct did not take. No appeal is made to their character as individuals.

(D) is also Outside the Scope because it widens the focus of the argument to corruption, but the captain's argument focuses only on graft.

(E) is incorrect because the problem with the argument is that the evidence isn't enough to establish the conclusion, not that the evidence and conclusion contradict each other.

19. (B) Paradox

Step 1: Identify the Question Type

The phrase "most helps to resolve the apparent paradox" - indicates a Paradox question.

Step 2: Untangle the Stimulus

In each region of the economist's country, the average full-time hourly wage went up last year. However, for the country as a whole, the same average wage decreased over the same time period.

Step 3: Make a Prediction

Perhaps more jobs were added in lower-paying regions of the country as compared to higher-paying regions. Whatever

occurred, the correct answer has to explain how the country's overall average full-time hourly wage decreased despite an increase in that average wage for each region.

Step 4: Evaluate the Answer Choices

(B) resolves the paradox. If employers moved more jobs from higher-paying regions of the country to lower-paying regions, then there were fewer jobs at the highest earning levels, thereby depressing the overall hourly wage.

(A) means that the decrease in the overall full-time hourly wage is part of a three-year trend, but that doesn't explain the contradiction with the increase in last year's regional average.

(C) doesn't explain the discrepancy because it's Outside the Scope. The unemployment rate doesn't have a strong enough relationship to the average full-time hourly wage.

(D) comes close to explaining the discrepancy, but it needs to demonstrate that the higher-paying regions saw a smaller rate of wage growth than did the lower-paying regions.

(E), in order to resolve the paradox, would require us to know the relative distribution and frequency of manufacturing jobs versus service sector jobs. The stimulus doesn't provide this information.

20. (E) Inference

Step 1: Identify the Question Type

This is an Inference question because it asks for the "conclusion ... most strongly supported by the information." This means that the right answer must be true given the stimulus.

Step 2: Untangle the Stimulus

In a comparison of the brains of recently deceased people with schizophrenia to those of recently deceased people without the disorder, a significant percentage of the former showed damage to a brain structure. This damage must have occurred while these people's brains were developing in utero.

Step 3: Make a Prediction

Putting all these statements together, the stimulus suggests that prenatal damage to a structure of the brain could contribute to the development of schizophrenia later in life.

Step 4: Evaluate the Answer Choices

(E) is therefore correct. Note the qualified language of this answer choice. The stimulus doesn't prove that prenatal damage to the subplate causes schizophrenia, but it certainly *may be* a cause.

(A) is Extreme. It extrapolates the statistical results of the study to the population at large, but without a whole lot more information, you can't determine that (A) "will eventually" be true.

(B) moves Outside the Scope from potential causes of schizophrenia to effective treatments, a leap that doesn't sustain a valid inference. No information is given regarding whether the subplate can be repaired, and even if it can, that the outlook for that treatment is *promising*.

(C) isn't supported by the stimulus, which only discusses subplate damage that occurred before the second fetal trimester. After that point, the stimulus doesn't provide any information to infer **(C)**.

(D) is Outside the Scope. It's safe to say from the stimulus that prenatal damage to the subplate could contribute to schizophrenia, but that doesn't necessarily mean that such damage has to arise from genetic factors.

21. (B) Strengthen

Step 1: Identify the Question Type

The phrase "support the prediction" indicates a Strengthen question.

Step 2: Untangle the Stimulus

The device's maker predicts that ranchers will buy the GPS device at its current price. This prediction comes despite the fact that outfitting all the cattle in a herd with the device is far costlier than other means of restricting cattle movement. The device works by making noises in a cow's ears when it strays outside its pasture.

Step 3: Make a Prediction

In order to strengthen the argument, the correct answer must make the prediction more likely to come true. In this case, ranchers need to be incentivized to purchase a device that's more expensive. The correct answer will describe some benefit of the new GPS device that outweighs its cost.

Step 4: Evaluate the Answer Choices

(B) supports the prediction by suggesting that only a few cattle need to be outfitted with the new GPS device. If the right few cattle are outfitted, then the rest of the herd will follow them back to the home range when the device is triggered, and ranchers don't need to shell out lots of money to outfit the whole herd.

(A) doesn't affect the argument because the device's maker predicts that ranchers will buy the device "at its current price," not at the promise of some future lower price.

(C) removes one possible objection to buying the device (animal cruelty), but **(C)** still doesn't make it any more likely that ranchers will fork over the extra money for the device.

(D) equates the device's effectiveness with that of fences, but because fences remain cheaper, **(D)** doesn't support the prediction that ranchers will buy the new device at the higher price.

(E), like **(A)**, introduces a condition that could lower the price of the device, but the device's maker predicts sales "at its current price."

22. (C) Parallel Flaw

Step 1: Identify the Question Type

This is a Parallel Flaw question because the reasoning in the stimulus is flawed, and the correct answer choice will be an analogous argument with the same flawed reasoning.

Step 2: Untangle the Stimulus

The Keyword *therefore* signals the conclusion: it's more economical to shop at a food co-op than at a supermarket. The evidence is that food co-ops are a type of consumer cooperative, and consumer cooperatives usually offer the same products as other stores but at cheaper prices.

Step 3: Make a Prediction

Notice the word *usually* in the stimulus. Consumer cooperatives *usually* offer cheaper products than other stores do, but not always. So, it could just as easily be true that food co-ops are unusually expensive or that supermarkets are unusually cheap. Put simply, the correct answer choice will compare a member of category A to a member of category B on the basis of what is *usually* (but not necessarily *always*) true about the categories as a whole.

Step 4: Evaluate the Answer Choices

(C) matches the stimulus exactly. Members of category A (users of private transportation) "tend to generate more pollution per mile" than category B (users of public transportation). However, to conclude that every member of category A (e.g., bicyclists) creates more pollution per mile than every member of category B (e.g., public bus users) is flawed in the same way as the stimulus.

(A) would need to be different in two ways to be parallel. If it concluded that a specific sports car used more gasoline *per mile* than another car that wasn't a sports car, then it would be parallel. But **(A)** doesn't delineate specific members of its categories, and it draws a conclusion about total gas usage based on evidence about gas usage per mile. Thus, it doesn't match the conclusion in the stimulus.

(B) fails on several points. First, **(B)**'s evidence doesn't say that frozen vegetables are *usually* better than fresh vegetables in those respects—there needs to be a qualifier like the one in the stimulus. Additionally, to be parallel it would need to have brought up individual members of each group rather than focus on the groups themselves. Finally, **(B)** brings up an additional consideration (spoilage) to determine which type of vegetable is *better*, whereas the stimulus focuses on just cost in the conclusion and evidence. So, to fix those issues, a parallel statement would be that it was *cheaper* (not better) to buy a frozen eggplant than to buy a fresh tomato, since fresh vegetables are *usually* more expensive than frozen ones.

(D) entirely misses the stimulus's assumption that a member of a group can be definitely compared to a member of another group based on a comparison that usually holds true.

(E) states its conclusion as a superlative ("the best way to lose weight") rather than comparing two alternative ways of losing weight in the same way that the stimulus compares two food stores. Also like **(B)**, there is no qualifier similar to *usually* in **(E)**'s evidence.

23. (C) Assumption (Sufficient)

Step 1: Identify the Question Type

This is a Sufficient Assumption question because the editorial's conclusion will follow logically *if* the correct answer is assumed.

Step 2: Untangle the Stimulus

The editorial concludes that it's wrong to blame the railroad company, even in part, for accidents that occur when drivers go around the gates that bar them from crossing railroad tracks. The evidence proceeds by making a distinction between this situation, in which licensed drivers are adults capable of higher decision-making, and a situation in which one has a duty to keep a small child from endangerment.

Step 3: Make a Prediction

The evidence says drivers are adults who should know better, and the conclusion says that these drivers therefore can't blame the railroad company for accidents. This conclusion is fully established if it's true that capable adults who willfully go around protective gates are completely responsible for any ensuing accidents.

Step 4: Evaluate the Answer Choices

(C) is therefore correct.

(A) doesn't help establish the editorial's conclusion that the railroad company is not to blame in this instance. In fact, **(A)** doesn't touch on the issue of culpability at all.

(B) might be correct if the editorial were attempting to distribute responsibility between the railroad company and the automobile driver, but the editorial in fact claims that drivers who go around the company's gates and cross the tracks indemnify the railroad company against any fault.

(D) mashes together two concepts from the argument. Small children are used as part of an example of a situation in which the responsibility for accidents may fall to the party restricting access; these children have nothing to do with drivers at railroad crossings.

(E) doesn't establish the editorial's conclusion. The editorial claims that the railroad company is not even partially

responsible for accidents, so it's not enough to assume simply that the company's responsibility is limited.

24. (E) Flaw

Step 1: Identify the Question Type

Because the stimulus says the "reasoning in the . . . argument is questionable," you know this is a Flaw question. Furthermore, you know to be on the lookout for an overlooked possibility.

Step 2: Untangle the Stimulus

The researcher concludes that a well-constructed survey's results will not be affected by respondents' desire to meet the surveyors' expectations. The evidence is twofold: some surveys don't accurately reflect respondents' views because people give answers they think the surveyor wants to hear, but well-constructed surveys are worded such that respondents can't determine what the surveyor expects to hear.

Step 3: Make a Prediction

The researcher makes the faulty assumption that survey respondents will refrain from entertaining beliefs about surveyors' expectations just because the respondents aren't given any indication of what those expectations are. In other words, the researcher overlooks the possibility that respondents will use their made-up beliefs about surveyors' expectations to answer the survey's questions.

Step 4: Evaluate the Answer Choices

(E) matches the prediction.

(A) is irrelevant to the researcher's argument because the researcher never claims that such well-constructed surveys are flawless. The claim is merely that these surveys' results won't be affected by respondents' ideas about what the surveyors expect them to say.

(B) isn't the overlooked possibility here because the researcher's argument is concerned primarily with people whose answers *are* likely to be influenced by the surveyors' expectations.

(C) is irrelevant to the argument because the researcher is concerned with people's beliefs about their surveyors' expectations, not whether or not those expectations actually exist.

(D) isn't a flaw in the argument because the argument is concerned with people who do want to meet their surveyors' expectations.

25. (A) Parallel Reasoning

Step 1: Identify the Question Type

The phrase "reasoning ... is most similar to" indicates a Parallel Reasoning question.

Step 2: Untangle the Stimulus

The conclusion of the argument comes in the first sentence: the availability of television reduces the amount that children read. The evidence is a couple of correlations: without television available, reading increases. But once television is reintroduced, reading levels drop back to their previous amounts.

Step 3: Make a Prediction

Your first task in abstracting the argument is to characterize its conclusion. Here, the conclusion is an assertion of fact; namely, an assertion of a causal relationship. The evidence is also statements of fact that assert correlation. The correct answer will use the same type of evidence to reach the same type of conclusion.

Step 4: Evaluate the Answer Choices

(A) is a parallel argument. Its first two sentences are correlations that support the conclusion (signaled by [*thus*) that a constant money supply leads to stable interest rates.

(B) does provide a causal conclusion, but the evidence is not parallel. It would be parallel if it provided evidence that the absence of candy is correlated with a healthy appetite and that the reintroduction of candy is correlated with a disrupted appetite. But the evidence doesn't match this.

(C) has a conclusion that states a causal relationship, but its evidence also establishes causal relationships—unlike the correlations in the stimulus—so **(C)** is not fully parallel.

(D) concludes that factors other than the one in question affect a certain outcome (not an exact match to the causal conclusion in the stimulus) and backs up this conclusion with two examples, a tactic the stimulus never employs.

(E), like the stimulus, concerns a decline in reading. But it's the two arguments' structures, not their subject matter, that make them parallel. The evidence in **(E)** would be a match if it said that the absence of activities coincided with a boost in adult reading and that the availability of activities coincided with a drop in reading. So, **(E)**'s evidence is not parallel because it only discusses when reading time is low and because it focuses on the time spent on activities rather than the availability of the activities.

Section II: Reading Comprehension
Passage 1: Video Technology and Indigenous Cultures

Q#	Question Type	Correct	Difficulty
1	Global	C	★
2	Inference	A	★
3	Logic Reasoning (Parallel Reasoning)	B	★
4	Detail	C	★
5	Detail	A	★
6	Inference	D	★
7	Inference	E	★★

Passage 2: Handling Judicial Bias

Q#	Question Type	Correct	Difficulty
8	Detail	B	★★
9	Logic Function	A	★★
10	Inference	A	★★
11	Inference	C	★★
12	Inference	B	★★
13	Inference	C	★★
14	Inference	E	★★★

Passage 3: Eye for an Eye

Q#	Question Type	Correct	Difficulty
15	Global	C	★
16	Detail	A	★★
17	Logic Reasoning (Method of Argument)	D	★★★
18	Inference	C	★★
19	Inference	E	★★
20	Logic Reasoning (Strengthen)	B	★★★★

Passage 4: Does Solid Glass Flow?

Q#	Question Type	Correct	Difficulty
21	Global	E	★
22	Detail	B	★★
23	Inference	A	★★★
24	Inference	D	★★★★
25	Detail	B	★★★
26	Logic Reasoning (Parallel Reasoning)	B	★★
27	Inference	C	★★★

Passage 1: Video Technology and Indigenous Cultures

Step 1: Read the Passage Strategically

Sample Roadmap

line #	Keyword/phrase	¶ Margin notes
5	struggling … even more …	indig. people filming own cultures
6	profound … Because	
12	sharply divided	Anthropologists divided
13	One faction	1st group (Weiner)
15	final assault	
16	argues	Video – Western culture
20	believes	
21	inevitably	Weiner: video robs indig. culture
23	Thus … concludes … costs	
25	Moreover … maintains	
28	naive	
29	But … opponents contend	2nd group (Ginsburg)
31	One such	
32	concedes	
34	but	
37	Unlike … maintains	
40	In fact	Ginsburg: video doesn't make indig. Western
41	believe … especially	Ginsburg: video helps indig. people preserve culture
42	invaluable opportunity	
47	lends credence	Turner's work supports Ginsburg
48		Kayapo use of video
50		
52	In contrast	Kayapo contradict Weiner
60	not so at odds	

Discussion

The passage begins by describing a recent phenomenon: cheaper video equipment has become available to indigenous cultures, and now those cultures, which were previously subject to documentation by Western ethnographic filmmakers, have begun to turn the cameras on themselves. The last sentence of paragraph 1 notes that reaction to this phenomenon among Western anthropologists is "sharply divided." Reading this sentence actively, you can probably guess that the passage will go on to detail this division.

Paragraph 2 outlines the position of "one faction" in the debate and identifies its leader, James Weiner. The position of Weiner et al. is that video technology is inherently Western in its ethos and that by using such technology, indigenous peoples lose what made them culturally distinct in the first place. By now, the **Topic** (the use of video technology by native peoples) and **Scope** (the debate over the impact of this technology) should start to become apparent.

Paragraph 3 begins with the Contrast Keyword [*b*]*ut*, signaling a shift to the other faction in the debate. This faction is represented by Faye Ginsburg, who argues that Weiner's position is reductive; simply picking up a video camera doesn't infuse the holder with Western cultural conventions. Ginsburg argues the opposite: video technology can help indigenous societies strengthen their native languages and traditions.

Paragraph 4 introduces evidence to support Ginsburg's position. Terence Turner's fieldwork with the Kayapo people has shown that video representations of Kayapo traditions conform to the same principles as the traditions themselves and provide an aesthetic mirror to their ceremonies. The **Purpose** of the passage is therefore to outline the debate among anthropologists concerning video's impact on native peoples and to share evidence that supports one side in the debate. The **Main Idea** is that there are two distinct schools of thought about how video technology has affected indigenous cultures, but some evidence supports the latter school.

1. (C) Global

Step 2: Identify the Question Type

This is a Global question because it asks for the answer choice that "completely summarizes the passage."

Step 3: Research the Relevant Text

The entire text is relevant because this is a Global question, so base your prediction on the Main Idea you determined during Step 1.

Step 4: Make a Prediction

The main point of the passage is that anthropologists disagree over the impact of video technology on native

cultures, but fieldwork exists to support the idea that indigenous people don't lose their culture just by using video technology.

Step 5: Evaluate the Answer Choices

(C) is therefore correct.

(A) only encapsulates the view of Weiner and those in his camp. It doesn't take into account any of paragraphs 3 and 4.

(B) distorts the first paragraph of the passage. Yes, ethnographers have attempted to eliminate the "colonial gaze," but the passage focuses on a different transformation of their discipline. Furthermore, nothing in the passage states that the "colonial gaze" has been eliminated successfully.

(D) doesn't take into account the argument presented in paragraph 2 or the evidence presented in paragraph 4.

(E) is Extreme. Turner's fieldwork doesn't conclusively *validate* the position of Ginsburg. Moreover, the Scope of the passage is the debate itself, not the evidence concerning the Kayapo people.

2. (A) Inference

Step 2: Identify the Question Type

This is an Inference question because it asks you to characterize the attitude of someone in the passage toward something mentioned in the passage.

Step 3: Research the Relevant Text

Paragraph 3 contains Faye Ginsburg's argument. Look for any language that compares or contrasts her with James Weiner.

Step 4: Make a Prediction

Line 31 characterizes Ginsburg as Weiner's *opponent*, suggesting that she fundamentally disagrees with his position.

Step 5: Evaluate the Answer Choices

(A) is therefore correct.

(B) is incorrect because nothing in the passage suggests that Ginsburg is reluctant to critique Weiner's ideas.

(C) is too timid. Line 35 says that Ginsburg calls Weiner's idea about video technology's effects "little more than boilerplate technological determinism." Hardly mild language.

(D) is incorrect because Ginsburg is not neutral when it comes to Weiner's position.

(E) is a 180. Ginsburg is not supportive of Weiner's position; in fact, she flatly disagrees with it.

3. (B) Logic Reasoning (Parallel Reasoning)

Step 2: Identify the Question Type

This is a Parallel Reasoning question because it asks for the answer choice "most analogous to" a portion of the passage.

Step 3: Research the Relevant Text

The Kayapo and their use of video technology are discussed in paragraph 4.

Step 4: Make a Prediction

Lines 47–60 describe the Kayapo's use of video to document their ceremonial performances. These representations "conform to the same principle of beauty embodied in the ceremonies themselves." The correct answer will be an example of a culture appropriating the tools of another culture while retaining the features that make their own culture unique.

Step 5: Evaluate the Answer Choices

(B) is a good match.

(A) is a 180. The Kayapo didn't move to another culture and alter that culture; the Kayapo incorporated one element of Western culture and used it to help preserve elements of their own society.

(C) is also a 180. The Internet is reshaping the way the authors write, but the Kayapo did not allow the camera to reshape their culture.

(D) is not analogous to the passage because the Kayapo were not imitating any cultural features from an earlier time. Historical homage doesn't figure into the Kayapo's use of video.

(E) is not parallel because the European artists are rejecting elements of their own culture and moving in a different direction. The Kayapo are taking devices from an outside culture in service of their own.

4. (C) Detail

Step 2: Identify the Question Type

The phrase "according to the passage" is a clear indication of a Detail question.

Step 3: Research the Relevant Text

Weiner's claims are detailed in paragraph 2. Specifically, "Western ontology" is mentioned in line 21.

Step 4: Make a Prediction

Line 22 says that according to Weiner, Western ontology is "based on realism, immediacy, and self-expression."

Step 5: Evaluate the Answer Choices

(C) is therefore correct.

(A) is mentioned as a feature of traditional Kayapo ceremonies (lines 54–59).

(B) is mentioned as something Weiner says anthropologists naively ascribe to films made by indigenous cultures (lines 25–28).

(D) is mentioned in line 2 as a characteristic of early ethnographic films.

(E) is a characteristic Weiner imputes to anthropologists who find ethnographic films culturally truthful simply because they were made by native peoples.

5. (A) Detail

Step 2: Identify the Question Type

This is a Detail question because it asks about which information is provided by the passage.

Step 3: Research the Relevant Text

Without any specific content clues, the entire passage is relevant, so save your research for Step 5.

Step 4: Make a Prediction

The passage provides enough information to answer a whole slew of questions. So, instead of predicting them all, check each answer choice against the passage.

Step 5: Evaluate the Answer Choices

(A) is answered in lines 50–52. The Kayapo use video technology to create legal records so they can hold the Brazilian government to the agreements it makes with the Kayapo.

(B) is not answered in the passage. The idea of the "noble savage" is mentioned in lines 30–31, but the passage doesn't say where the idea came from.

(C) is not answered. The only specific indigenous culture mentioned is the Kayapo, and the passage says that they have adopted video technology.

(D) is not answered. Ginsburg concedes in lines 32–34 that no Western cultural object that has entered circulation since the fifteenth century has remained neutral, but no specific technologies from that time are mentioned.

(E) is not answered. Line 7 confirms that inexpensive video equipment is now more available, but the author never says how the equipment became inexpensive.

6. (D) Inference

Step 2: Identify the Question Type

This is an Inference question because it asks what Turner "would most likely to agree with."

Step 3: Research the Relevant Text

Terence Turner's research is discussed in paragraph 4. Within that paragraph, Weiner is mentioned in lines 52–53.

Step 4: Make a Prediction

Turner's findings contradict Weiner's position that video technology imposes Western culture on its users. Therefore, Turner would believe that Weiner's position doesn't allow for instances in which native peoples could use Western technology but still preserve their own unique cultural identity.

Step 5: Evaluate the Answer Choices

(D) is therefore correct.

(A) is Outside the Scope because Weiner makes no argument that depends on the *diversity* of traditional practices among native peoples.

(B) is not a position Turner would take regarding Weiner's argument because even if video technology is *available* worldwide, Turner is more concerned with Weiner's argument that indigenous cultures will be altered as a result.

(C) is not a position Turner would take regarding Weiner's argument because Weiner seems to demonstrate concern for preserving traditional indigenous practices. In fact, that concern underlies Weiner's suspicion of video technology.

(E) is not something Turner would likely agree with because Weiner's position has more to do with video's effect on native peoples rather than the effect of Western technologies in general.

7. (E) Inference

Step 2: Identify the Question Type

This is an Inference question because it asks what an author means by using a particular term. Therefore, the correct answer will not be directly stated, but must be inferred.

Step 3: Research the Relevant Text

Line 35 is relevant, of course, but to grasp the author's full meaning, you must read the surrounding lines for context.

Step 4: Make a Prediction

In line 35 and the surrounding lines, the author summarizes Ginsburg's position on Weiner's claims. Ginsburg considers it "technological determinism" to say that using a video camera automatically makes one Western. In other words, "technological determinism" refers to the idea that technology determines the cultural identity of indigenous peoples.

Step 5: Evaluate the Answer Choices

(E) is therefore correct.

(A) might be tempting if you use the dictionary definition of "determinism." But in the context of the passage, "determinism" has more to do with Weiner's idea that cultures are altered by their use of technology.

(B) mischaracterizes the influence of video technology. The debate is about the influence of video on native cultures, not about its influence on field anthropologists.

(C) uses a meaning of "determinism" that might be familiar to biologists, but in the context of this passage, it doesn't reflect

Weiner's argument about native peoples' relationship to video technology.

(D) introduces the idea of a culture's ethical values, an idea which is Outside the Scope of both Weiner's and Ginsburg's arguments.

Passage 2: Handling Judicial Bias

Step 1: Read the Passage Strategically

Sample Roadmap

line #	Keyword/phrase	¶ Margin notes
1	current	Current approach to
2	heavily emphasizes	recusal based on
4	avoidance of both	appearances
12	vague ... at best	Auth: rules vague
15	without	
16	mistake	
17	focus on	Auth: shouldn't focus on appearances
18	rather than	
24	overlooked	bias overlooked
26	only if	Justice occurs thru reasoning
29	Therefore ... best way	
30	require	Auth: judges should explain reasoning
31	Accordingly ... should	
32	eliminate	
33	unreliable	
34	should ... replaced by ... requirement	
38	should not	
40	but rather ... should be required	
43	potential objection	Objection: judge's reasoning not "real"
44	however ... adequate	
45	thus	
46	However	Auth: if no fault in reasoning no complaint
49	only if	
50	If	
53	then	

Discussion

This Law passage begins by summarizing the current approach to recusal and disqualification of judges, which "heavily emphasize appearance-based analysis." Judges are expected to recuse themselves in instances of impropriety or even the appearance of impropriety. Jurisdictional rules vary regarding whether or not parties to a court can themselves request recusal. You can expect this author to express a point of view about these rules, and that point of view comes in paragraph 2.

Paragraph 2 lays out the author's position: the current rules are "vague ... at best." In the author's view, it's a mistake to focus too much on appearances at the expense of discovering sources of actual bias. Such bias may not be apparent to the parties to a court proceeding or even to judges themselves, so appearance-based analysis provides a shaky foundation on which to base ethical rules.

Paragraph 3 provides the author's suggestion for a revision of the rules. Instead of focusing on the appearance of impropriety, rules governing judicial ethics should focus on the reasoning behind a judge's ruling. Judges should be required to make such reasoning transparent. If judges recuse themselves, they should explain why, and if they do not, they should explain the legal basis for the judgment they reach.

In paragraph 4, the author anticipates a potential objection to this recommendation. Some might allege that the judge's written reasoning is not the real reasoning used to reach a decision. *However*, the author contends, there are no grounds for complaint if the legal reasoning is deemed sound by a knowledgeable observer. If another objectively impartial judge could have reached the same legal conclusion as the judge in question, then no harm is done.

This is a relatively challenging Law passage, but sticking closely to the author's point of view can help you sort it out. The **Topic** is judicial bias, and the **Scope** is approaches to setting rules for handling such bias. The author's **Purpose** is to critique the current approach and propose a new approach. The **Main Idea** is that our legal system should replace the current appearance-based approach with an approach focused on a judge's underlying legal reasoning.

8. (B) Detail

Step 2: Identify the Question Type

The phrase "[a]ccording to the passage" indicates a Detail question.

Step 3: Research the Relevant Text

"A weakness of current rules" is a content clue leading you to paragraph 2, where the author critiques the current approach to recusal and disqualification of judges.

Step 4: Make a Prediction

Lines 12–16 say that the current rules provide "vague guidance at best" and that they fail to provide an idea of whose perspective matters or how the facts should be interpreted.

Step 5: Evaluate the Answer Choices

(B) is therefore correct.

(A) is a Distortion. Judges' reasoning isn't discussed until the author recommends a new approach in paragraph 3.

(C), like **(A)**, introduces judicial reasoning, which is part of the author's recommendation. Furthermore, paragraph 3 indicates that the author highly values transparency in judicial reasoning.

(D) is mentioned as a feature of the recusal rules in some jurisdictions (lines 10–11). But the author doesn't directly criticize this feature.

(E) is a 180. The author says in paragraph 2 that the current rules focus too much on the appearance of propriety.

9. (A) Logic Function

Step 2: Identify the Question Type

This is a Logic Function question because it asks you to determine the "primary purpose" of part of the passage.

Step 3: Research the Relevant Text

The second paragraph is relevant, but in order to form your prediction, consult your margin notes rather than rereading the entire paragraph.

Step 4: Make a Prediction

Paragraph 2 provides the author's evaluation of the current approach to recusal that was discussed in paragraph 1.

Step 5: Evaluate the Answer Choices

(A) is therefore correct.

(B) is a Distortion. The author's solution is provided in paragraph 3, and it is never rejected anywhere in the passage.

(C) is incorrect because the author doesn't discuss any problems in the first paragraph. Furthermore, no examples of such problems are given in the passage.

(D) is a 180. Far from being an objective discussion of the history leading to the current approach, the author uses paragraph 2 to take issue with the current approach.

(E) is a Distortion. The author's own thesis doesn't occur until paragraph 3.

10. (A) Inference

Step 2: Identify the Question Type

This is an Inference question because it asks how an author *regards* something mentioned in the passage. Don't worry if you thought this might be a Detail question; you would execute Steps 3 and 4 in largely the same way.

Step 3: Research the Relevant Text

Lines 49–50 are relevant, as well as the context of the surrounding lines.

Step 4: Make a Prediction

The author says that the principle that a right of recourse arises only if harm arises is a principle "under the law." Furthermore, it's a principle on which the author bases a rebuttal to a potential objection to the recommendation made in paragraph 3. The author must therefore consider this principle fairly ironclad.

Step 5: Evaluate the Answer Choices

(A) is consistent with the way the author uses the principle to further the passage's argument.

(B) misuses a point from lines 25–26, in which the author says that the law's function is to settle "normative disputes."

(C) is a Distortion. The principle in lines 49–50 is why it's *not* a concern that judges might hide their real reasoning.

(D) is a 180. If this principle were unfair to parties to legal proceedings, then the author would not have used the principle to support the passage's Main Idea.

(E) is a Distortion. The principle in lines 49–50 has nothing to do with the *current* means of addressing judicial bias, which is discussed in paragraphs 1 and 2. The principle in lines 49–50 instead relates to the author's proposed solution.

11. (C) Inference

Step 2: Identify the Question Type

The phrase "can be inferred from the passage" is a clear indication of an Inference question.

Step 3: Research the Relevant Text

The author primarily discusses "weakness of statutes" in paragraph 2.

Step 4: Make a Prediction

In paragraph 2, the author faults the current rules for basing disqualification on a vague standard of "whether the judge's impartiality might reasonably be questioned." According to the author, no guidance is given as to whose perspective to consult or how to interpret the facts of the case.

Step 5: Evaluate the Answer Choices

(C) is consistent with lines 22–24.

(A) is a 180. The author says at the beginning of paragraph 2 that the rules concerning recusal and disqualification provide "vague guidance at best." So, they are certainly not "excessively rigid."

(B) is a Distortion. The author does suggest requiring judges to make their reasoning transparent, but there's no indication that this requirement is incompatible with current rules.

(D) is a 180. Rather than conflicting with statutes allowing people to request disqualification of judges, the professional codes of conduct mentioned in **(D)** likely form the basis for these statutes.

(E) can't be inferred because the author makes no prediction concerning the outcomes of potential requests for disqualification.

12. (B) Inference

Step 2: Identify the Question Type

Any question that asks about what the passage "suggests" is an Inference question.

Step 3: Research the Relevant Text

The author recommends that judges be required to provide their written legal reasoning at the end of paragraph 3, and further support for this recommendation comes in paragraph 4.

Step 4: Make a Prediction

In paragraph 4, the author says that the judge's reasoning is acceptable "as long as a knowledgeable observer cannot find fault" with it. This provision is intended to respond to critics who allege that judges might not be giving their real reasoning.

Step 5: Evaluate the Answer Choices

(B) is a valid inference. If faulty reasoning cannot in principle be detected, then the author would presumably have refrained from making the recommendation in lines 40–42.

(A) is Extreme. The author mentions earlier in the passage that sources of bias are not always apparent, so it's hard to conclude that bias can be *eliminated* altogether.

(C) is a 180 because it is an objection that the author anticipates and seeks to counter in lines 46–54. Additionally, even if some situations arise where judges attempt to conceal their reasoning, the passage does not suggest that that would be the *usual* practice of judges.

(D) is Outside the Scope. The author isn't concerned with public perception of judges' impartiality. The author is instead concerned with ways to ensure that bias doesn't affect the outcome of cases.

(E) is a 180 because the author argues against recusal when there is only an "appearance of bias." The author would not have proposed a solution where judges must provide written legal reasoning if the effect would be to cause recusals based merely on an appearance of impropriety.

13. (C) Inference

Step 2: Identify the Question Type

This is an Inference question because it asks you to find the answer choice that is "an example of" something mentioned in the passage. The correct answer won't be stated directly by the author, but will instead be consistent with the passage.

Step 3: Research the Relevant Text

Lines 43–46 are of importance here, but be sure to read around these lines for context.

Step 4: Make a Prediction

The "real reasoning" referred to in these lines is reasoning that might not be reflected in a judge's official written explanation of a decision. In other words, this "real reasoning" could actually reflect a judge's bias against a party to a court proceeding.

Step 5: Evaluate the Answer Choices

(C) is therefore a valid inference. The reasoning described in (C) is the kind of reasoning that could conceal a judge's "undetected bias" (line 46).

(A) is unsupported. The author says in lines 38–39 that judges should not be required to explain why they chose not to recuse themselves.

(B) is Outside the Scope. The "undetected bias" mentioned in line 46 has nothing to do with whether or not a judge's reasoning can be understood by laypeople.

(D) is a Distortion. The author says that a knowledgeable observer should not be able to find fault with a judge's stated reasoning in explaining a decision, not in that judge's concealed and potentially biased "real reasoning."

(E) is a Distortion. The author makes a distinction between the reasoning contained in a judge's written explanation, which should be based on legal principles, and potential "real reasoning," which can be based on bias.

14. (E) Inference

Step 2: Identify the Question Type

The looser language in this question stem ("author would be most likely to consider") indicates an Inference question.

Step 3: Research the Relevant Text

The author analyzes the effects of the current approach to recusal and disqualification in paragraph 2.

Step 4: Make a Prediction

The author says that it's a mistake to base the current approach to recusal and disqualification primarily on appearances, which can be deceiving. That focus on appearances, says the passage, could lead jurists to miss actual sources of bias. Line 33 even calls the current system an "unreliable mechanism."

Step 5: Evaluate the Answer Choices

(E) is consistent with the "unreliable mechanism" described in the passage.

(A) is Outside the Scope. The author doesn't discuss the attitudes of the general public toward the current standards.

(B) is also Outside the Scope. The author doesn't say how judges personally feel about their professional codes of conduct. The effects of the current system are of primary importance to the author.

(C) is a Distortion. The author never suggests a difference between how often unbiased judges are removed from cases and how often biased ones are allowed to sit on cases.

(D), like (C), suggests that the author gives an indication of how frequently judges are removed from cases in certain instances, but no such indication exists in the passage.

Passage 3: Eye for an Eye

Step 1: Read the Passage Strategically

Sample Roadmap

line #	Keyword/phrase	¶ Margin notes
Passage A		
1–3		
4	lower standards	Augustine: 2 wrongs don't make a right
5	yet … indeed	Auth: may be just to repay lies with lies
6	some justification	
8	:	
11	Just as	Lying to liars—fairness
12	so	
14	Two	2 moral Qs involved
15	first	
17	second	
21	Surely	Exception: pathological liar
23	But … not … sufficient	tall tales don't justify lying
Passage B		
28	holds	
32	That is	Kant: rational beings authorize repayment of behavior
34	Consequently	
38	might be concluded	Kant argument could mean duty to punish
41	But	
42	seems excessive … since	Auth: duty too extreme
46	The point … rather	
49	leads to	
50	rather than	Auth: Kant argument means right, not duty

Discussion

Passage A begins by offering the view of Saint Augustine, who believed that one shouldn't respond to a liar by lying. In Augustine's view, two wrongs never make a right. In paragraph 2, the author gives the counterpoint: some see responding to lies by lying as inherently just. The author doesn't offer her own point of view on this debate, but instead outlines two questions involved in the debate. One question asks whether a liar and an honest person have the same claim to be told the truth, and the other asks whether one is more justified in lying to a liar than to others.

Passage A ends with a case study in which it may not be justified to reply to a liar with lies. If the liar in question is pathological, meaning that he compulsively tells tall tales that are harmless, lying in response to him may actually do a disproportionate amount of harm to "self, others, and general trust." The **Topic** of passage A is lying, the **Scope** is whether it's justified to repay lies with lies, the **Purpose** is to discuss the debate over whether such lying is justified, and the **Main Idea** is that while many believe it is justified to repay lies with lies, other considerations may affect that justification in certain cases.

Passage B begins by outlining Kant's view that rational beings, by virtue of their rationality, authorize others to behave toward them as they themselves behave. So, according to Kant, to respond in kind to a rational person's immoral behavior is merely part of treating that person as a rational being.

In the second paragraph, the author takes this logic one step further. If we feel we should treat rational beings as rational, then we might conclude that Kant's argument saddles us with a duty to repay bad behavior with similarly bad behavior. But, says the author, that might be going too far. Instead, Kant's argument leads to a right, not a duty. If a rational being behaves immorally, we then have a right to respond as that rational being has implicitly authorized us to do.

The **Topic** of passage B is Kant's view of reciprocal behavior. The **Scope** is the implications of that view. The **Purpose** is to discuss and evaluate those implications. The **Main Idea** is that Kant's argument leads us to conclude that we have a right, but not a duty, to behave toward rational beings as they behave toward us.

On Comparative Reading passages, always note areas of overlap between the passages; the questions are sure to ask about them. In this case, both passages explore whether it is justified to repay an improper action with a similarly improper action. Passage A, however, restricts its discussion to the practice of lying, while passage B explores immoral actions in general.

15. (C) Global

Step 2: Identify the Question Type

This is a Global question because it asks what both passages are "concerned with answering."

Step 3: Research the Relevant Text

The entire text is relevant to a Global question. Use your work from Step 1 to predict the answer here.

Step 4: Make a Prediction

The passages overlap in their discussion of whether it is proper to respond in kind to another person's wrongdoing.

Step 5: Evaluate the Answer Choices

(C) is therefore correct.

(A) is touched upon briefly in the last paragraph of passage A, but passage B doesn't discuss the idea of harm.

(B) is Outside the Scope. The idea of criminality doesn't appear in either author's analysis.

(D) is discussed in passage B, but not in passage A.

(E) is also discussed in passage B, but not in passage A.

16. (A) Detail

Step 2: Identify the Question Type

This is a Detail question because it asks about information introduced—that is, stated directly—in one or both passages.

Step 3: Research the Relevant Text

The question stem directs you to restrict your research to passage A only.

Step 4: Make a Prediction

Several considerations are introduced in passage A. Instead of predicting them all, check each answer choice against the passage.

Step 5: Evaluate the Answer Choices

(A) is discussed primarily in the last paragraph of passage A, in which the author asserts that one may do unwarranted harm by lying in response to the lies of a person whose behavior is known to be pathological.

(B) is a Distortion. Passage A discusses the consequences that can ensue when people do reciprocate another's wrongdoing, but not the ones that ensue when people do *not* reciprocate.

(C) is a 180. It is not mentioned in A, but it is mentioned in passage B where the author discusses how Kant viewed rational beings.

(D) is also discussed in passage B, but not in passage A.

(E) is a Distortion. Neither passage offers specific *instances* of harm done to people whose wrongdoing was reciprocated.

The discussion of the pathological liar in lines 19–27 is merely hypothetical.

17. (D) Logic Reasoning (Method of Argument)

Step 2: Identify the Question Type

This is a Method of Argument question because it asks how each passage advances its argument.

Step 3: Research the Relevant Text

Both passages are relevant in this case, but instead of rereading them, use your Roadmap and your global understanding of the passages to predict your answer.

Step 4: Make a Prediction

Each passage explores a view concerning the reasonableness of responding to wrongdoing with wrongdoing, and then shows how unreasonable implications can result from that view.

Step 5: Evaluate the Answer Choices

(D) is therefore correct.

(A) is a Distortion. Neither author argues against any objections to a particular theory.

(B) is incorrect because neither author bases a main argument on an analogy. Saint Augustine uses an analogy in lines 1–2 of passage A, but this is not how either author structures either passage as a whole.

(C) is incorrect because even if you consider the pathological liar in passage A to be a specific case, passage B contains no such case but rather remains abstract in its discussion.

(E) is incorrect because neither passage attempts to redefine a key term.

18. (C) Inference

Step 2: Identify the Question Type

This is an Inference question because it asks what an author "would be most likely to agree with."

Step 3: Research the Relevant Text

Passage A is the only passage relevant here.

Step 4: Make a Prediction

You may not be able to predict the correct answer verbatim, but the correct answer will be compatible with passage A's Main Idea that it may not always be justified to repay a liar with lies.

Step 5: Evaluate the Answer Choices

(C) is a valid inference. Passage A says that a liar may have forfeited his or her right to be told the truth (lines 12–13, 21–22), but in certain cases, it might not be justified to lie to that person (lines 23–27).

(A) is within the scope of passage B. Passage A doesn't discuss rational beings.

(B) is Outside the Scope of passage A, which concerns only how to respond to wrongdoing—not how to respond to actions that are morally neutral.

(D) is almost a 180. Passage A suggests that it may be justified to respond to a wrong with a similar wrong (lines 11–13). The specific case of the pathological liar does indicate one case where it would be *improper* to respond in kind, but it would be extreme to say there is "no circumstance in which there is sufficient reason."

(E) is Outside the Scope. Nothing in passage A suggests that an *innocent* person forfeits the right to be dealt with honorably.

19. (E) Inference

Step 2: Identify the Question Type

This is an Inference question because it asks you to "characterize the difference" between a concept in passage A and one found in passage B.

Step 3: Research the Relevant Text

The lines cited in the question stem are relevant, but be prepared to read around those lines to get a sense of context.

Step 4: Make a Prediction

Lines 11–13 describe an inherent right to be treated well by others, a right that one forfeits by doing wrong. Line 50 describes a right to treat others poorly in response to their own wrongdoing.

Step 5: Evaluate the Answer Choices

(E) is therefore correct.

(A) is Half-Right, Half-Wrong. Both passages discuss moral rights; the law doesn't enter into the discussion.

(B) is a Distortion. Nothing in passage B suggests that the right to treat others poorly in response to their own wrongdoing is a right granted by any specific authority figure.

(C) is incorrect because in each passage, the kind of right referred to is one held by an individual, not held by a group.

(D) is a 180. Passage A discusses a kind of right that can readily be forfeited by those who do wrong.

20. (B) Logic Reasoning (Strengthen)

Step 2: Identify the Question Type

This is a Strengthen question because it asks you to find the answer choice that, if true, makes arguments from the two passages compatible.

Step 3: Research the Relevant Text

Both the last paragraph of passage A and the first paragraph of passage B are relevant in this case.

Step 4: Make a Prediction

In the last paragraph of passage A, the author argues that a pathological liar's tall tales don't on their own justify lying to him because the harm done to him by lying to him outweighs the negligible harm of his tall tales. In passage B, Kant argues that rational beings implicitly authorize reciprocal treatment when they act immorally. These arguments are compatible if it were demonstrated that a pathological liar is somehow outside the realm of rationality.

Step 5: Evaluate the Answer Choices

(B) is therefore correct.

(A) is a Distortion and Outside the Scope. Lying in response to a pathological liar is not in itself pathological, and Kant's argument concerns whether the *original* bad behavior comes from a rational being. The rationality of *our* response to that behavior doesn't figure into the argument.

(C) is a 180. If pathological liars should be treated as rational beings, then, according to Kant's argument, it would in fact be justified to respond to those liars with lies of our own, an idea that contradicts the argument at the end of passage A.

(D) supports passage B's author's view regarding the implications of Kant's argument, but doesn't reconcile that argument with the one laid out in passage A.

(E) certainly bolsters Saint Augustine's argument from the beginning of passage A, but it does nothing to reconcile passage A's author's argument with that of Kant in passage B.

Passage 4: Does Solid Glass Flow?

Step 1: Read the Passage Strategically

Sample Roadmap

line #	Keyword/phrase	¶ Margin notes
1	strange	
3 – 4		Wrong belief: window glass flows
8	but … confusion … probably	
9	misunderstanding	why people believe this
12	but	
14	rather	Glass has transition temp
18	but	
20	However … debunks	Zanotto's study debunks belief
25	But	Zanotto's calculation
31		More of Zanotto's findings
36		
37	but	
38	since	
39	demonstrates	Zanotto's study supports scientists views
40	dramatically	
45	probably results … instead	Auth: changes in manufacturing methods true cause
46	Until	
53	Later	Auth traces changes in glass manufacturing
55	Today	

Discussion

Don't be thrown by the arcane subject matter of this Natural Sciences passage. Like many passages of this type, this passage outlines a commonly believed explanation for a phenomenon, presents evidence undermining that explanation, and suggests an alternative explanation. In this case, the common belief has to do with the perceived viscosity of glass. The variations in thickness of old window glass have often been thought to be the result of glass flowing very slowly over time. The second half of paragraph 1 outlines the basis of this misperception. Many people misunderstand the atomic structure of glass. This structure is similar from liquid glass to solid glass, but these different phases of glass diverge when it comes to thermodynamics. Rather than a precise freezing point, glass has what's known as a transition temperature, and once molten glass is cooled below the lower end of that range, it begins to take on the physical properties of a solid. By now, it should become clear that the **Topic** is glass, and the **Scope** is explanations for why glass thickness can vary within the same antique window.

Paragraph 2 begins with the Contrast Keyword [*h*]*owever*, signaling a shift. Here, the author introduces Zanotto's study, which debunks the persistent belief mentioned earlier. The author concedes that gravity can cause some solids to flow slightly. But Zanotto calculated the time it would take for us to perceive the flow of solid glass, and that time period amounts to longer than the age of the universe.

Paragraph 3 provides more information gleaned by the study. Chemical composition can alter the rate of flow of glass, but only slightly, and certainly not enough to be noticeable after only a handful of centuries (which is the age of medieval stained-glass windows). Zanotto's study lends statistical credence to the position already held by scientists.

Now that the "persistent belief" has been thoroughly called into question, the author uses paragraph 4 to provide an alternative explanation. Rather than a viscous flow, changes in manufacturing methods are the reason why antique window glass displays differences in thickness from top to bottom. The rest of the paragraph lays out a few of those changes from before the nineteenth century all the way to today. The **Purpose** of the passage is therefore to supplant a commonly held belief about why glass thickness varies in older glass. Therefore, the **Main Idea** is that differences in thickness in old window glass are explained not by the properties of glass itself, but by changes in how glass has been manufactured over the centuries.

21. (E) Global

Step 2: Identify the Question Type

This is a Global question because it asks for the "main point" of the passage.

Step 3: Research the Relevant Text

You already determined the Main Idea of the passage during Step 1. Use that as the basis for your prediction.

Step 4: Make a Prediction

The main point of the passage is that the difference in thickness between the top and bottom of glass windowpanes is better explained by the manufacturing process than by the flowing of glass.

Step 5: Evaluate the Answer Choices

(E) is therefore correct.

(A) just reiterates the second half of paragraph 2. But Zanotto's calculations are only provided to support the larger point that window glass has not flowed enough to cause a noticeable difference in thickness from top to bottom.

(B) is a point made in paragraph 4, but that point only serves to help explain the author's broader position concerning why glass varies in thickness.

(C) describes Zanotto's discovery, but that discovery is not the focus of the passage. Zanotto is only mentioned to help debunk the commonly held belief with which the author takes issue.

(D) misrepresents the author's point of view. According to paragraph 4, there aren't several factors explaining the difference in thickness between the top and bottom of old windows; the author points to only one factor.

22. (B) Detail

Step 2: Identify the Question Type

This is a Detail question because it deals with what the passage explicitly mentions. The correct answer choice will be a question directly answered by the information in the passage.

Step 3: Research the Relevant Text

There are no content clues here, so the entire passage is relevant text. Save your research for Step 5.

Step 4: Make a Prediction

It's nearly impossible to predict the correct answer to a question like this one, so check each answer choice against the passage, using the content clues within them to pinpoint the relevant text.

Step 5: Evaluate the Answer Choices

(B) is answered in paragraph 4. Lines 46–52 describe how glass was made before the nineteenth century. The Keyword [*l*]*ater* in line 53 signals a shift to the nineteenth century, which is contrasted in lines 55–57 with the approach to glassmaking [*t*]*oday*.

(A) is not answered by the passage. Lines 46–52 describe the glassmaking process and indicate that there was an "only way" to do it until the nineteenth century. No distinctions were made between different periods leading up to the nineteenth century.

(C) is not answered by the passage. Medieval windows are the earliest ones discussed in the passage.

(D) is not answered by the passage. Germanium oxide glass is mentioned at the beginning of paragraph 3 as a type of glass that flows relatively easy, but it's not stated that this glass was used in stained-glass windows.

(E) is not answered by the passage. Line 35 states that medieval stained glass contains impurities, but no information is given as to how those impurities came about.

23. (A) Inference

Step 2: Identify the Question Type

This is an Inference question because it asks about the author's view, or attitude, toward part of the passage.

Step 3: Research the Relevant Text

The results of Zanotto's study are discussed in the end of paragraph 2 and throughout paragraph 3.

Step 4: Make a Prediction

Because the author uses the results of Zanotto's study to discredit the belief held by laypeople that glass viscosity accounts for the difference in thickness between the top and bottom of old windows, you can properly infer that Zanotto's findings support the author's view. Furthermore, the last sentence of paragraph 3 says that Zanotto's study demonstrates what many scientists had already reasoned.

Step 5: Evaluate the Answer Choices

(A) matches the prediction.

(B) is a 180. Scientists can't have thought the issue had been settled because the author says that glass researchers find it strange that the myth about flowing glass persists (lines 1–4).

(C) is a Distortion. The author explains in paragraph 1 how the mistaken hypothesis about window glass came to be believed. Zanotto's study doesn't figure into that discussion.

(D) is incorrect because there aren't two incompatible views that the author attempts to reconcile. Rather, the author spends the passage undermining one explanation for a phenomenon and endorsing another.

(E) is another Distortion. There are two hypotheses to explain the phenomenon discussed in the passage, but according to the author, one of them is valid and supported by evidence.

24. (D) Inference

Step 2: Identify the Question Type

This is an Inference question because it asks about what "the passage suggests." That looser language means that the correct answer won't be stated directly, but rather supported by the passage.

Step 3: Research the Relevant Text

The atomic structure of glass is discussed in paragraph 1, specifically in lines 8–19.

Step 4: Make a Prediction

According to the passage, the atomic structure of glass remains constant in its amorphousness from solid to liquid states. However, solid and liquid glass differ thermodynamically. At any temperature above the lower range of the glass transition temperature, molten glass retains the properties of a liquid.

Step 5: Evaluate the Answer Choices

(D) is a valid inference.

(A) is a Distortion. The last few lines of paragraph 1 indicate that glass does not always behave as a liquid.

(B) warps a detail from paragraph 2 about the length of time needed to perceive the flow of glass. That length of time is described as "a period well beyond the age of the universe" (lines 29–30), not simply a few millennia.

(C) is a Distortion because paragraph 1 says that molten glass behaves as a solid when it is cooled below the lower range of its glass transition temperature. That suggests that at this transition temperature, it still behaves as a liquid.

(E) isn't a valid inference because the passage describes conditions under which glass will flow, despite the fact that its atoms are not arranged in a fixed crystalline structure.

25. (B) Detail

Step 2: Identify the Question Type

This is a Detail question because it asks about something explicitly attributed by the author. The correct answer will state or paraphrase information already contained.

Step 3: Research the Relevant Text

The false belief that window glass flows noticeably downward over time is discussed in paragraph 1.

Step 4: Make a Prediction

Lines 7–10 say that the myth about glass originates from a misunderstanding of the atomic structure of glass. Because that structure is amorphous, people believe that even solid glass takes on the properties of a viscous liquid.

Step 5: Evaluate the Answer Choices

(B) is therefore correct.

(A) is a Distortion. No one mistakenly believes that glass has a fixed crystalline structure. Rather, the author says that people misinterpret the implications of the amorphous atomic structure of glass.

(C) is another Distortion. The mistaken belief about glass has nothing to do with the changes in manufacturing methods; those changes are instead at the heart of the author's own attempt to counter this mistaken belief.

(D) is incorrect because paragraph 1 suggests that all glass has the same transition temperature. The author doesn't attempt to debunk any inaccurate beliefs about transition temperatures.

(E) is incorrect because liquid and solid glass are actually thermodynamically dissimilar, according to the passage (lines 12–13). So, this is not an erroneous assumption.

26. (B) Logic Reasoning (Parallel Reasoning)

Step 2: Identify the Question Type

The phrase "most analogous to" indicates a Parallel Reasoning question.

Step 3: Research the Relevant Text

"Persistent belief" is a content clue leading you to lines 1–7.

Step 4: Make a Prediction

The persistent belief discussed in the passage is the belief that the difference in thickness between the top and bottom of old windows is explained by the viscous flow of glass. The correct answer probably won't mention glass at all; instead, it will describe a similar belief, namely that a phenomenon is explained by properties of the material itself rather than manufacturing methods.

Step 5: Evaluate the Answer Choices

(B) is a perfect match. The "early pottery" mentioned in **(B)** parallels the old windows discussed in the first lines of the passage.

(A) is a Distortion. The manufacturing process has more to do with the author's explanation and less to do with the belief cited at the beginning of the passage. Furthermore, the belief in the passage seeks to provide a cause for a phenomenon, not to predict whether that phenomenon can be changed.

(C) might be parallel if it said that people blamed the materials used to make appliances—rather than the manufacturing techniques—for the shorter life spans of those appliances. However, even in that scenario, the varying level of thickness in window glass is not commensurate with a flaw causing a window to have a shorter life span.

(D) is incorrect because the persistent belief in the passage is about a certain phenomenon. **(D)** merely compares two different types of material and deems one inferior.

(E) might be parallel if the passage said that people believe that newer windows don't have differences in thickness because their glass is more durable. But the persistent belief in lines 1–7 doesn't compare older glass to newer glass.

27. (C) Inference

Step 2: Identify the Question Type

"The passage suggests" is a clear sign of an Inference question.

Step 3: Research the Relevant Text

The transition temperature of glass is mentioned primarily in lines 13–19.

Step 4: Make a Prediction

The passage defines the glass transition temperature as a range of a few hundred degrees Celsius within which glass transforms its physical properties from those of a liquid to those of a solid. However, Celsius is also mentioned in lines 41–43, which state that in order for glass to noticeably flow, it must be heated to at least 350 degrees Celsius.

Step 5: Evaluate the Answer Choices

(C) is a valid inference. The temperature of 350 degrees Celsius is mentioned in paragraph 3 as the lowest temperature to which glass would have to be heated to flow noticeably. In other words, it's the lowest end of the transition temperature, at which glass takes on the properties of a liquid. Therefore, it is strongly supported that the upper extreme of the transition temperature is well above 350 degrees.

(A) is a comparison with no basis in the passage. The author suggests that the age of glass is irrelevant to its transition temperature.

(B) is a Distortion. Zanotto has calculated the amount of time it would take for glass to flow noticeably, but nothing in the passage details when and how precisely the glass transition temperature has been calculated.

(D) is unsupported by the passage, which says that once molten glass is cooled below the lower end of the transition temperature, it stops flowing and takes on the properties of a solid. Therefore, the transition temperature *does* affect the tendency of glass to flow downward.

(E) isn't a valid inference because nothing in the passage suggests that certain types of glass have more precise transition temperatures than others. Furthermore, lines 41–43 indicate 350 degrees Celsius is the minimum for glass in general, so there wouldn't be any types below 350 degrees Celsius.

Section III: Logical Reasoning

Q#	Question Type	Correct	Difficulty
1	Inference	C	★
2	Assumption (Necessary)	B	★
3	Principle (Identify/Strengthen)	C	★
4	Inference	D	★
5	Paradox	A	★
6	Strengthen	B	★
7	Flaw	B	★
8	Main Point	C	★
9	Parallel Reasoning	E	★★
10	Flaw	C	★★
11	Method of Argument	E	★★★
12	Strengthen	B	★★
13	Weaken	C	★★★★
14	Parallel Flaw	D	★★
15	Assumption (Sufficient)	E	★★
16	Flaw	A	★
17	Assumption (Necessary)	B	★★★
18	Flaw	E	★★
19	Assumption (Necessary)	C	★★★★
20	Role of a Statement	D	★★★
21	Strengthen	E	★★★
22	Weaken (EXCEPT)	A	★★★
23	Assumption (Necessary)	A	★
24	Inference	B	★★
25	Assumption (Necessary)	A	★★★★

1. (C) Inference

Step 1: Identify the Question Type

The correct answer will fill in the blank at the end of the given argument. The Keyword [o]*bviously* indicates that the last sentence, including the blank, will logically follow from the information before it. That means the last sentence is a supported inference.

Step 2: Untangle the Stimulus

New technology is presenting a lose–lose situation here. When companies adopt new technology, people who can master it do well. The rest lose their jobs. When companies *don't* adopt new technology, they become obsolete and *all* their employees lose their jobs.

Step 3: Make a Prediction

The blank will be the *obvious* conclusion regarding companies that resist new technology. According to the evidence, those companies will lose out to other companies, and employees will all lose their jobs. The correct answer will be consistent with this rather bleak outcome.

Step 4: Evaluate the Answer Choices

(C) cuts right to the idea of inevitable job loss.

(A) is a 180. Dislocated workers are the *more* likely scenario as employees lose their jobs.

(B) is a Distortion and a 180. Those who possess technical skills only retain their jobs in businesses that *apply* new technology. In industries that *resist* technology, *everyone* is affected.

(D) is a 180. Jobs will be lost, not created.

(E) is Out of Scope and a possible 180. The author is merely talking facts, and there's no support for a recommended course of action. Even if there were, resisting technology is going to lead to job loss—hardly an action that should "take priority over" anything.

2. (B) Assumption (Necessary)

Step 1: Identify the Question Type

This question directly asks for an assumption, which is said to be *required* by the argument. That makes this a Necessary Assumption question. The correct answer must be true for the conclusion to follow from the evidence.

Step 2: Untangle the Stimulus

Sales of the Hydro, a fuel-efficient vehicle, are increasing while sales of other fuel-efficient vehicles are going down. The Hydro's manufacturer attributes this to the Hydro's great price and low fuel consumption. The Keyword [h]*owever* indicates the author's disagreement. The author claims that the Hydro and its competitors have pretty much the same price and fuel consumption. The Keyword *so* indicates the

author's alternative conclusion: the great sales are due to something else: people wanting to show off how environmentally friendly they are.

Step 3: Make a Prediction

In determining why the Hydro's sales are so different from those of other fuel-efficient vehicles, the author is justified in rejecting two factors that are *not* different among the competing vehicles. However, why choose people's desire to look good for the neighbors as the difference-maker? The author doesn't even consider other potential factors, assuming that keeping up appearances is the one likely to affect sales. Furthermore, the author rejects price and fuel consumption because of their similarity among vehicles, but never actually says there's something *different* about the Hydro that helps people appear more environmentally friendly. There *must* be a difference to claim that as a cause of higher sales.

Step 4: Evaluate the Answer Choices

(B) must be true. After all, using the Denial Test, if the Hydro is *not* seen as being different from its competitors, then the author has no reason to cite appearances as a contributing factor.

(A) is Extreme. The Hydro does not have to be the *most* popular. Its sales can increase even while far more popular vehicles have slight dips in their sales.

(C) is an Irrelevant Comparison and a 180. A better safety record is irrelevant and would, if anything, provide an alternative explanation for sales that doesn't involve mere appearances.

(D) is a Distortion. The author's point is about people wanting to appear environmentally friendly; it's not about them wanting to own the same thing as their neighbors.

(E) is a Distortion and a possible 180. There's a difference between actually *being* interested in the environment and wanting to *appear* interested. At worst, if Hydro buyers don't really care about the environment, it's harder for the author to justify attributing sales to their wanting to appear environmentally friendly.

3. (C) Principle (Identify/Strengthen)

Step 1: Identify the Question Type

The question asks for a principle that will *justify*, or strengthen, the author's judgment. So, this is an Identify the Principle question that mimics a Strengthen question. The correct answer will support the author's reasoning in broad terms.

Step 2: Untangle the Stimulus

A homeowner is trying to file a complaint with the Licensing Bureau against a nightclub. She was supposed to use a particular form, but someone at the Licensing Bureau gave her a different form, and she used that one instead. The nightclub wants the complaint dropped because the wrong form was used. The author disagrees (indicated by the Keyword [*b*]*ut*), claiming this would not be fair.

Step 3: Make a Prediction

Specifically, the author says it would be unfair to dismiss the homeowner's complaint, even though she clearly used the wrong form. The only evidence that could back up the author's judgment is that the homeowner was *given* the wrong form by the Licensing Bureau itself. The correct answer will generalize this: if somebody uses the wrong form because it was *given* to her, then it's not fair to dismiss the complaint.

Step 4: Evaluate the Answer Choices

(C) generalizes the circumstances exactly, thus supporting the author's claim.

(A) is Out of Scope. There's no evidence whether the homeowner was informed of the regulations or not. It's possible she was informed but was still given the wrong form.

(B) is Out of Scope. The author never mentions how difficult any of the forms are to fill out.

(D) is Out of Scope. The Bureau staff gave the homeowner the wrong form, but that doesn't necessarily indicate a lack of understanding of the procedures. It could have been a simple mistake.

(E) is Out of Scope. The question asks for justification as to why it's unfair for the homeowner, not why it's unfair for the business. Furthermore, there's nothing that suggests the nightclub wasn't allowed to defend itself anyway.

4. (D) Inference

Step 1: Identify the Question Type

The correct answer will be "supported by the information above," which means this is an Inference question. Look for ways to connect statements and make logical deductions.

Step 2: Untangle the Stimulus

Two general relationships are presented. Sickly birds have smaller spleens than healthy birds, and predators tend to kill birds with smaller spleens than those killed by accident.

Step 3: Make a Prediction

If predators tend to kill birds with smaller spleens and smaller spleens usually indicate more sickly birds, it stands to reason that predators tend to kill birds that are more sickly.

Step 4: Evaluate the Answer Choices

(D) makes the logical connection between what predators kill and the birds' health.

(A) is Extreme. Predators kill birds with smaller spleens (i.e., sickly birds) "in general." That hardly means they're *unable* to kill healthy birds.

(B) is also Extreme. Predators may kill lots of birds with smaller spleens, but there could still be countless more such birds that escape. Most such birds may survive after all.

(C) is Out of Scope. There's no evidence that the predators can *sense* sickness. Perhaps sickly birds are just slower and make easier targets.

(E) is an Extreme Distortion. What's described is merely a correlation between spleen size and sickness. There's no indication of causality, let alone whether spleen size would be a *main* cause.

5. (A) Paradox

Step 1: Identify the Question Type

The stimulus will provide an "apparent conflict," which the correct answer will *resolve*. Solving the mystery behind a conflict is the hallmark of a Paradox question.

Step 2: Untangle the Stimulus

As expected with a Paradox question, there's something *surprising*. In this case, home ownership is supposed to indicate economic prosperity, but unemployment is high in various regions where home ownership is prevalent.

Step 3: Make a Prediction

So, the mystery can be summarized simply as this: why would regions with so much home ownership—that should be home to economically prosperous residents—experience such high levels of unemployment? It's not worth predicting an exact explanation, but expect the correct answer to provide a reason why people struggle to find jobs in a good economy.

Step 4: Evaluate the Answer Choices

(A) could resolve the issue. Even though the economy of the region overall is great and there are plenty of jobs, unemployment is high because homeowners don't live near those jobs and would struggle to move closer.

(B) is a 180. If the jobs were moving *closer* to homeowners, the mystery deepens. Why are so many people still unemployed?

(C) is Out of Scope. If different social systems don't affect the level of unemployment, then the question still remains: why is unemployment so high in these regions?

(D) is a 180. If homeowners are more likely to help each other find jobs, it's even *less* clear why they're still unemployed.

(E) is a Distortion. This might explain the first piece of information: why home ownership is a sign of economic prosperity. However, that doesn't address the central conflict about why unemployment is so high in these cases.

6. (B) Strengthen

Step 1: Identify the Question Type

The correct answer "adds ... support," or strengthens, the given reasoning. Find the conclusion, which is said to be a *hypothesis*, and look for an answer that validates the assumption leading to that conclusion.

Step 2: Untangle the Stimulus

The hypothesis here is meant to explain the unusual eating habits of the tobacco hatchworm. If the first thing it feeds on after hatching is a nightshade plant, then that's the only type of plant it will ever eat. Otherwise, it's not as picky. The hypothesis is that this is due to a chemical found only in nightshade plants: indioside D. Once the worm tastes it, the worm's taste buds adapt to the chemical and everything else tastes terrible.

Step 3: Make a Prediction

The hypothesis is based on the suggested effect of the chemical on the worm's taste receptors. No other explanations are even suggested. That means the scientists are rejecting other possibilities, assuming that the eating habits are solely based on the chemical and taste. The correct answer will provide further evidence that the chemical and/or taste play a role in the worm's eating habits.

Step 4: Evaluate the Answer Choices

(B) provides some helpful evidence. If nightshade-eating hornworms *with* taste receptors keep eating nightshade plants, but nightshade-eating hornworms *without* taste receptors eat other plants, then that strengthens the hypothesis that taste receptors are a factor in the eating habits.

(A) is an Irrelevant Comparison. The argument is about why such worms would prefer nightshade plants over *non-nightshade* plants, not about any preference among different varieties of nightshade plants.

(C) is Out of Scope. The frequency of eggs being laid on nightshade plants would indicate *how often* hornworms develop the eating habits described, but the hypothesis is about *why* the worms have such eating habits.

(D) is a 180. If nightshade plants contain other unique chemicals, then there's reason to believe that even if taste is still a factor, it's something *other* than indioside D that plays a role.

(E) doesn't actually help, and could even be a 180. Even if the taste receptors react to *several* chemicals, that's not enough to suggest that indioside D is one of those chemicals. Even if that were the case, this would still create doubt by suggesting there may be explanations other than indioside D.

7. (B) Flaw

Step 1: Identify the Question Type

The question asks why the given argument is *flawed*, making this easily identified as a Flaw question. Look for an answer that describes why the evidence does not adequately back up the conclusion.

Step 2: Untangle the Stimulus

The employee was given some feedback about a presentation: it should have had more detail. The Keyword [*s*]*o* expresses the employee's conclusion: this is wrong. There was no reason for more detail. The evidence is that too much detail would cause an audience to lose interest.

Step 3: Make a Prediction

The employee is right to worry about *too much* detail, but the boss merely requested *more*. There could have been room to add more detail without going overboard, but the employee fails to consider that—and that's the flaw in the argument.

Step 4: Evaluate the Answer Choices

(B) directly points out the employee's unwarranted leap from "more detail" to "too much detail."

(A) is Out of Scope. The employee is only rejecting one assessment about detail, not necessarily making any commentary or assumptions about the boss's assessments in general.

(C) is a Distortion. Even if there were other ways to lose an-audience's attention, too much detail would still cause the audience's minds to wander—and the employee would be perfectly justified in wanting to avoid that.

(D) gets the logic backward. The employee rejects the assessment in a single case (advice on the employee's presentation) based on a generalization ("people's attention tends to wander") about what affects audiences in general.

(E) suggests the flaw of equivocation. However, the word *detail* is used consistently throughout the argument. It always refers to information (e.g., stats or data).

8. (C) Main Point

Step 1: Identify the Question Type

The question asks for the "overall conclusion," so this is a Main Point question. Look for the one claim that is supported by everything else.

Step 2: Untangle the Stimulus

The author starts with information about the media being proven wrong for touting the scandal-involved politician Clemens as honest. This information is then used to *demonstrate* a point: local media is often too deferential toward public figures. As further evidence, the author cites a newspaper editor who confessed that reporters ignored leads that could have exposed Clemens earlier.

Step 3: Make a Prediction

All of the information about Clemens consists of facts and details (i.e., evidence). These merely serve as a specific example to support (or, as the Keyword indicates, *demonstrate*) the author's broader main point (i.e., conclusion): local media show too much deference toward public figures.

Step 4: Evaluate the Answer Choices

(C) is the central point of the argument.

(A) is merely an established fact from the first sentence, not a conclusion.

(B) is a fact from the second sentence. However, that fact is used to *demonstrate* the broader point about media's treatment of public figures in general.

(D) is the fact in the last sentence, but it's still part of the specific situation that demonstrates the author's broader point about the local media in general.

(E) is implied, but it doesn't express the author's stated conclusion that there's "too much" of this kind of behavior.

9. (E) Parallel Reasoning

Step 1: Identify the Question Type

The correct answer will be an argument with reasoning "similar to" that of the given argument. That indicates a Parallel Reasoning question. Compare structural components, and find the answer that reaches the same type of conclusion using the same logic as the stimulus.

Step 2: Untangle the Stimulus

The given argument is based on Formal Logic. If there were ever life on the Moon, there would be signs. However, we have never found any signs, so there must never have been life there.

Step 3: Make a Prediction

The author basically uses a contrapositive to reach the conclusion:

If	life on Mars	→	signs
If	~ signs	→	~ life on Mars

However, the reasoning is not quite that sound. The conclusion is concrete ("there has *never* been life on the Moon"), but the evidence just states we haven't *found* any signs. That doesn't mean the signs don't exist. Even though this question isn't presented as a Parallel Flaw question, the correct answer should still follow the same questionable format: if an event were to occur (life on Moon), there would

be evidence (signs). We haven't *seen* that evidence, so the event doesn't happen.

Step 4: Evaluate the Answer Choices

(E) matches the logic exactly. if an event were to occur (army plans an attack), there would be evidence (troop movements or weapons transfer). We haven't *seen* that evidence, so the event doesn't happen.

If	planning an attack	→	troop movements OR transfer of weapons
If	~ troop movements AND ~ transfer of weapons	→	~ planning an attack

Again, the same unsound reasoning applies: intelligence reports don't indicate troop movements or weapon transfers, but that doesn't mean they haven't actually happened.

(A) falls apart immediately by presenting a known piece of evidence ("We know that the spy is a traitor"). Nothing was known in the original argument. Also, there's no Formal Logic here.

(B) has Formal Logic, but the conclusion is qualified ("it is unlikely") rather than unjustifiably strong. Also, the evidence is different. Instead of citing a lack of evidence (e.g., "there's no sign of mayonnaise"), it merely says the refrigerator is *almost* empty.

(C) fails on a couple of levels. For starters, "will probably go" in the conclusion doesn't denote the same unwarranted strength as the original stimulus. Also, the terms in the Formal Logic don't exactly match: *Hendricks's* view on criminal penalties is not an exact match of *voters'* concern with fighting crime.

(D) has the Formal Logic: If an event were to occur (rodents affecting harvest), there would be evidence. However, instead of citing a lack of evidence to kick off a contrapositive, the author states that they *have* found evidence and concludes that the event *did* occur.

If	rodents responsible	→	signs
If	signs	→	rodents responsible

This argument improperly confuses necessity and sufficiency (i.e., it reverses without negating – a necessary versus sufficient flaw). However, that was not a problem with the original argument.

10. (C) Flaw

Step 1: Identify the Question Type

The correct answer will describe why the given argument is *flawed*, making this easy to spot as a Flaw question.

Step 2: Untangle the Stimulus

The phrase "I still believe" is a clear indication of the host's conclusion: the defendant is still guilty, despite a strong alibi, evidence of innocence, and an acquittal. And what evidence does the host have? Merely the fact that the prosecutor brought up charges in the first place.

Step 3: Make a Prediction

So, despite all of the evidence to the contrary, the host is still siding against the defendant based on the opinion of one person: the prosecuting attorney. However, opinions are just that—opinions. Without actual evidence to contradict the acquittal, the alibi, and everything else, the host's reliance on the prosecutor's actions are dubious at best.

Step 4: Evaluate the Answer Choices

(C) correctly exposes the host's reliance on an authority figure (the prosecutor) rather than having any actual evidence.

(A) is a Distortion. The host does conclude that a view (the defendant is innocent) is false. However, there *is* plenty of evidence for the defendant's innocence.

(B) suggests circular reasoning. However, the host's argument is based on what the prosecutor did, so the host's evidence and assumptions—although still flawed—are not merely a repeat of the conclusion.

(D) is Out of Scope. The argument is solely about legal guilt. Moral standards are never addressed.

(E) is a Distortion. While it *is* said that the defendant was "quickly acquitted," that's not the host's reason for doubting the judgment. The host dismisses the judgment because of the prosecutor's actions.

11. (E) Method of Argument

Step 1: Identify the Question Type

This is certainly an unusual question stem. However, when analyzed carefully, it's merely asking for the professor's argumentative strategy, i.e., *how* the professor presents the argument. So, this is a Method of Argument question. As an added benefit, the question already provides half the answer: the professor argues that the critics haven't properly established their point. The correct answer will complete the thought by expressing the *grounds*, or evidence, for the professor's claim.

Step 2: Untangle the Stimulus

Critics argue that Sauk's works lack aesthetic merit because he uses the same style as another writer who would disagree with Sauk's political ideals. The professor concedes those points, but claims they have no effect on the craft of Sauk's writings. As indicated by the Keyword [s]o, the professor concludes that the critics are wrong.

Step 3: Make a Prediction

The last sentence is the professor's conclusion, which rejects the critics' claim (just as the question stem suggested). The *grounds* for this claim are presented immediately before it: even though the critics make valid points, those points can't be said to devalue the merit of Sauk's works. The correct answer will express that piece of evidence.

Step 4: Evaluate the Answer Choices

(E) accurately expresses the professor's reasoning. The critics may have good points, but they're not relevant. Sauk's works are still subtly and powerfully crafted.

(A) is a 180. The professor concedes the critics' points, agreeing that Sauk is an imitator with different political views.

(B) is a Faulty Use of Detail. This is what the professor is arguing, not the *grounds*, or evidence, in support of that argument.

(C) is a Distortion. While it *is* claimed that some critics would reject Sauk's political ideals, the professor never cites that as a motivation for their assessment.

(D) is another 180. The author admits that the critics' claims (Sauk's imitative style and different political views) are indeed correct. The professor just disagrees with the critics' assessment that Sauk's work lacks aesthetic merit.

12. (B) Strengthen

Step 1: Identify the Question Type

The stimulus presents a policy (usually associated with Principle questions), as well as an application of that policy. The application will be the conclusion based on the policy, which serves as the evidence. You don't need to broaden or narrow anything—just justify the application—which is why this is a Strengthen question rather than a Principle question.

Step 2: Untangle the Stimulus

The application concludes that a factory's safety inspector should reject a new welding process because there's no evidence that it will make things safer. This application is based on the Formal Logic of the policy:

If	new process approved	→	used for over a year at another factory OR shown to increase safety

Step 3: Make a Prediction

Approval requires a one-year testing cycle *or* a display of safety. Even though the new welding process failed to display safety, it could *still* meet the other requirement: the one-year test at another factory. To justify rejecting the new welding process, it should be shown that the process doesn't meet that other requirement. Essentially, the application formed the contrapositive, but didn't add the term before the *and* on the sufficient side.

If | ~ used for over a year at another factor AND ~ shown to increase safety | → | ~ new process approved

Step 4: Evaluate the Answer Choices

(B) fills in the missing gap. If the process wasn't used anywhere else at all, then it hasn't been used for more than a year. Add that to the evidence that it hasn't been shown to increase safety, and that's enough to say it shouldn't be approved.

(A) is Out of Scope. While problems may *sound* like a good reason to reject the process, the policy still allows acceptance under the condition that it was used somewhere else safely for more than a year. It doesn't necessarily matter what happened at the factory where it was *first* introduced. Perhaps there have been many other factories that have subsequently used it without incident for more than a year.

(C) is a Distortion and Out of Scope. This suggests that the new welding process is just as safe, if not *safer*, than some current processes. However, the policy only involves approving new processes, not about necessarily eliminating ones currently used. The processes that are currently used that are "not demonstrably safer" may be for tasks other than welding, and are thus irrelevant. The author's point goes unjustified because it's not known if the welding process was tested elsewhere.

(D) is Extreme and a Distortion. The question is only about the new welding process, not *any* new process. And besides, there's still no evidence about how much this new process was used elsewhere.

(E) is a Distortion. It doesn't matter how *many* other factories use the process. The requirement is based on how *long* it's been used elsewhere. Unless that one factory has been using it less than a year, this is not enough to reject the new process.

13. (C) Weaken

Step 1: Identify the Question Type

This question directly asks for something that weakens the given argument.

Step 2: Untangle the Stimulus

Grad students are complaining that TAs should be treated as and receive benefits like other university employees. The

Keyword [*h*]*owever* indicates the administrator's contrary point: the only reason TAs are used is to help them pay for college. The evidence is that TAs are solely students who couldn't otherwise pay for their education.

Step 3: Make a Prediction

While the TA population may consist entirely of students who need financial help, the administrator is making a rather strong claim that this is the *sole* reason for the TA program. This suggests that the university has no reason to use TAs other than generous altruism. Any answer that suggests an ulterior motive will undermine the administrator's argument.

Step 4: Evaluate the Answer Choices

(C) implies that TAs are being used to support the university's economic interest—hardly the selfless goal the administrator was boasting about.

(A) is irrelevant. The administrator's point is that the university is merely helping the TAs fund their education. Benefits are a nonissue, so it doesn't matter whether the administrator is aware of the benefits costs.

(B) is Out of Scope. The presence of adjunct faculty has no effect on why the university employs TAs.

(D) is a Distortion. The administrator states that TAs are paid to fund their *education*. Even if they're paid beyond *tuition* costs, the extra stipend may still be used for other educational purposes such as books or lab fees. In that case, the administrator's argument would still hold.

(E) is Out of Scope. The work ethic of TAs does not change the administrator's reasoning for hiring them in the first place.

14. (D) Parallel Flaw

Step 1: Identify the Question Type

The question directly asks for parallel reasoning that is described as *flawed*, so this is a Parallel Flaw question. The correct answer will not only have the same logical structure as the stimulus, but it will also contain the same logical flaw.

Step 2: Untangle the Stimulus

Branson points out that air pollution is most prevalent in large cities. So, Branson suggests moving people out of the large cities. That would reduce pollution in those cities, and thus reduce pollution in the country as a whole.

Step 3: Make a Prediction

Branson overlooks a fundamental issue: moving people out of the city doesn't eliminate pollution. The pollution will just move with people to the rural areas. So, pollution may go down in the city, but the overall level won't necessarily change. The correct answer will try to apply the same faulty logic: concluding that something will be reduced overall (pollution) by moving it from where it appears most (large cities) to someplace else (rural areas).

Step 4: Evaluate the Answer Choices

(D) makes the same mistake. It concludes that something will be reduced overall (caloric intake) by moving it from where it appears most (major meals) to someplace else (snacks). And just as Branson's country will still produce the same amount of pollution overall, Javier will still consume the same number of calories overall.

(A) doesn't match from the get-go. The conclusion is not about reducing something overall. It's a claim about "most of" something, which should be part of the evidence. **(A)** is flawed because although Monique is spending *more* on housing, it is unknown if she spends *most* of her salary on housing.

(B) talks about having *more* of something (living space), rather than reducing something. Regardless, the evidence isn't about moving that something from one place to another, so the logic doesn't line up. The logic of **(B)** is sound—not flawed—provided Karen's family has a typical apartment and would move to a typical single-family home.

(C) also stumbles immediately by not having a conclusion about reducing something overall. Again, this has a conclusion about "most of" something, which should be part of the evidence. **(C)** is flawed because it is unknown if Ward's farm is representative of the rest of the county. Although the county as a whole has switched most fields planted with other crops to corn, there's no guarantee that Ward's farm has followed suit. Furthermore, there's no information on what proportion of Ward's fields were planted with other crops to begin with. It's possible it's been untended or used as grazing land, so even a switch to corn for those fields that were planted, might not mean *most* of the farm is now planted with corn.

(E) again fails to present a conclusion about reducing something overall. And again, the conclusion is about "most of" something, which should be part of the evidence. **(E)** is flawed because although pollution would be reduced if people switched to public transportation, it is unknown if *most* pollution would be eliminated. Perhaps the majority of pollution was not related to transportation.

15. (E) Assumption (Sufficient)

Step 1: Identify the Question Type

The question asks for something that, *if* it were *assumed*, would complete the logic of the argument. That makes it a Sufficient Assumption question. The correct answer will logically close the gap between the evidence and the conclusion.

Step 2: Untangle the Stimulus

A lot of people claim that safety is an important factor in buying a car. However, of these people, only half researched objective safety details while the other half just looked at ads. The Keyword [*t*]*hus* indicates the author's conclusion: the latter half doesn't really consider safety all that important.

Step 3: Make a Prediction

The author makes quite a jump in logic. The evidence and conclusion are about the same group of people, but the evidence merely mentions their information source (nonobjective ads), while the conclusion judges their concerns about safety (they're not really concerned). The assumption will connect those concepts: people who don't research objective sources of safety aren't really concerned about safety. Or, to put it in contrapositive terms, people who *are* concerned about safety *do* research objective sources.

Step 4: Evaluate the Answer Choices

(E) makes the logical connection between safety concerns and the buyers' sources of information.

(A) is Out of Scope. This argument isn't concerned with what people would consider the *most* important factor in a buying decision.

(B) is a Distortion. Even if the promotional information is incomplete, the second group of people might think it's enough to make a sound judgment of safety. In that case, they *would* still be interested in safety, contrary to the author's point.

(C) is a Distortion. This suggests that some car buyers *may* not be telling the truth. However, it doesn't say which ones. It's possible that the ones who just check ads are still telling the truth, contradicting the author's point.

(D) is a Distortion. Even if people know the ads are subjective, they could still trust the ads and consider the safety information to be valid. In that case, they could still be telling the truth about their safety concerns.

16. (A) Flaw

Step 1: Identify the Question Type

The question is directly asking for the flaw in the argument. Be on the lookout for some commonly tests flaws.

Step 2: Untangle the Stimulus

The Keyword [*t*]*hus* indicates the author's conclusion: if an organism can't perform planned locomotion, it doesn't have a central nervous system. The evidence is that planned locomotion requires certain activities, which in turn require a central nervous system.

Step 3: Make a Prediction

By Formal Logic, the evidence states that organisms require a central nervous system for planned locomotion, meaning a central nervous system is *necessary*.

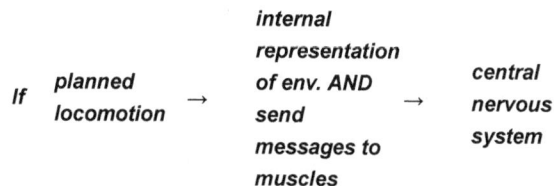

| If | planned locomotion | → | internal representation of env. AND send messages to muscles | → | central nervous system |

However, the author concludes that organisms *unable* to perform planned locomotion *don't* have central nervous systems.

| If | ~ planned locomotion | → | ~ central nervous system |

That logic by the author negates without reversing. By contrapositive of the faulty conclusion, that also means if it *did* have a central nervous system, it *could* perform planned locomotion.

| If | central nervous system | → | planned locomotion |

The author concludes that the central nervous system is *sufficient*. That's not supported by the evidence, making this a classic case of the author confusing necessity and sufficiency.

Step 4: Evaluate the Answer Choices

(A) indicates the author's all-too-common flaw.

(B) is a Distortion. It does work backward from the intermediate requirement of sending messages to muscles to the original sufficient statement of planned locomotion. However, there are a few inconsistencies. Nothing indicates that the messages to the muscles definitely come from the nervous system. Furthermore, this answer merely discusses locomotion, not necessarily *planned* locomotion. If any animals were capable of *unplanned* locomotion, the author makes no assumptions about them.

(C) is an Extreme Distortion. The author does mention that planned locomotion requires forming a representation of the environment, but never suggests that planned locomotion is the *only* useful result of such a representation.

(D) is Out of Scope. The author merely discusses what factors are involved in planned locomotion, not the reason such factors arose in the first place.

(E) is a Distortion. The author only makes assumptions about a *central* nervous system, not a *rudimentary* nervous system. Besides, the argument is about how it relates to planned locomotion, not the internal representation.

17. (B) Assumption (Necessary)

Step 1: Identify the Question Type

The question directly asks for an assumption, and one that that argument *requires*, making it a Necessary Assumption question.

Step 2: Untangle the Stimulus

Thus indicates the author's conclusion: all rockets need both short and long nozzles on the engines to work most effectively throughout their ascent. The evidence is that the different nozzle sizes work better at different pressures—short nozzles are best for the lower atmosphere (high pressure), and long nozzles are best for the upper atmosphere (lower pressure).

Step 3: Make a Prediction

Different nozzles would certainly work best on any rocket going through the different layers of the atmosphere. However, the author's conclusion is about *all* rockets. Do all rockets go through the different layers? That would have to be true for the author's argument to work.

Step 4: Evaluate the Answer Choices

(B) must be true. Consider the Denial Test. What if there were some rockets that *didn't* pass through the upper atmosphere; they just rose through the lower atmosphere, then descended. Those rockets would only need short nozzles, not long nozzles. The author's point would be invalid—not *every* rocket would need both nozzle sizes.

(A) is Out of Scope. The difficulty of installing the different nozzles doesn't matter. Even if they were harder to install, they could still be necessary.

(C) is a Distortion. The argument is not about whether a rocket *can* reach high altitudes, it's about how it can do so *most effectively*.

(D) is a subtle Distortion. This suggests that equal pressure between the nozzles and atmosphere is needed for the rocket to work effectively at all. However, that doesn't have to be true. The argument is about what would be *most* effective. Even if rockets worked effectively with single-size nozzles, the use of long and short nozzles could still be the *most* effective solution.

(E) is yet another subtle Distortion. The author claims that short and long nozzles both need to be present, but not necessarily on the same engines. Perhaps each rocket has multiple engines, with each engine used at different altitudes. In that case, the engines used at lower altitudes would need short nozzles while the other engines would need long nozzles. There wouldn't need to be any individual engine with both nozzles.

18. (E) Flaw

Step 1: Identify the Question Type

The question directly asks for the flaw in the consumer advocate's argument. Look for a reason why the evidence doesn't adequately back up the conclusion.

Step 2: Untangle the Stimulus

The Keyword [*t*]*herefore* indicates the conclusion: toy manufacturers shouldn't overstate the danger of their products. The evidence is that manufacturers are overstating dangers merely to protect themselves from lawsuits, and dangers should be overstated only if that will reduce injuries.

Step 3: Make a Prediction

The given principle is the key here: overstating dangers should be done *only if* it reduces injuries. To conclude that labels *shouldn't* overstate dangers, the author must be assuming that the warnings don't actually reduce injuries. But what if they *do*? What if, even though manufacturers aren't *trying* to reduce injuries (just trying to protect themselves), the labels *still* help reduce injuries anyway? The author overlooks that possibility, continuing to assume that injuries will not be reduced.

Step 4: Evaluate the Answer Choices

(E) needs to be translated a little, but gets to the core problem. The author does assume that an action (overstating dangers) would only have an effect (reduce injuries) if that were the motive. But because that's *not* the manufacturers' motive, the author assumes the labels won't have that effect.

(A) is a Distortion. The author never identifies anything necessary to reducing injury. Instead, the effect of reducing injury is itself a necessary condition for using labels with overstated dangers.

(B) is Out of Scope. This argument is only concerned with labels that *do* overstate dangers. It doesn't matter what happens with labels that *don't*.

(C) is Out of Scope. There is no sample. The evidence and conclusion are both about toys in general.

(D) is a Distortion. The author doesn't assume that labels that overstate dangers won't *prevent* injuries. The author just assumes that they won't necessarily *reduce* the number of injuries.

19. (C) Assumption (Necessary)

Step 1: Identify the Question Type

The question outright asks for an assumption, and one on which the argument *depends*, making this a Necessary Assumption question.

Step 2: Untangle the Stimulus

The author concludes, as indicated by [*t*]*hus*, that drinking tea boosted immune system defenses. The evidence is that the blood cells in people who drank only tea responded twice as fast to germs as blood cells in people who drank only coffee.

Step 3: Make a Prediction

Why did tea drinkers' blood cells act so much more quickly? The author assumes it must have had something to do with the tea. However, there could be another explanation. Alas, the author assumes otherwise—that nothing else (e.g., something about the coffee) was responsible for the discrepancy in blood cell response time.

Step 4: Evaluate the Answer Choices

(C) must be true. If everyone started out with the same response time, the author is implying response time got *faster* in tea drinkers. But what if, instead, the response time just got *slower* in coffee drinkers? Then the tea would have been ineffective, denying the author's reasoning. The author *must* assume that the coffee had no such effect. A quick check using the Denial Test rephrases (C) as "drinking coffee *did* cause the blood cell response time to double." If true, that would destroy the author's argument.

(A) is not necessary. The author only mentions the people who drank tea or coffee exclusively, but there could have been other people in the study who did drink both but were irrelevant to the author's argument.

(B) is Out of Scope. Other health benefits have nothing to do with whether the tea was responsible for the immune system response discrepancy.

(D) is Out of Scope. Using the Denial Test, even if coffee drinkers *did* have healthier lifestyles, the tea could still have been responsible for boosting immune defenses. This does not need to be true for the argument to work.

(E) is also Out of Scope. Even if tea has a unique chemical to boost immune defenses, that doesn't mean it can't share some other chemical with coffee that fights disease in some other way. Testing (E) with the Denial Test indicates that the two drinks *do* share a chemical that helps fight disease. That fact would in no way invalidate the author's conclusion about tea leading to improved immune response times.

20. (D) Role of a Statement

Step 1: Identify the Question Type

This question stem is rather long, but it's merely asking for "the role played" by a particular claim from the stimulus. That makes this a Role of a Statement question. Start by marking the claim in question in the stimulus. Then, break the argument down and consider *how* the marked claim fits within the structure.

Step 2: Untangle the Stimulus

The statement in question (about transportation being more expensive on monohulls than on regular ships) is the second sentence. As for the rest of the argument, the conclusion comes at the very end, indicated by the Keyword [*t*]*hus*: monohulls will be profitable. The evidence is that monohulls have advantages similar to jet planes, which were also able to be profitable despite how expensive it was to use them initially.

Step 3: Make a Prediction

The statement in question (travel on monohulls will be much more expensive) doesn't sound good for the author's conclusion about their potential profitability. However, the author then brings up the analogy to jet planes to show why that statement regarding cost won't necessarily affect profitability in the long run. The correct answer will express how the statement is presented as a possible problem that's explained away by the jet analogy.

Step 4: Evaluate the Answer Choices

(D) expresses the statement's role exactly.

(A) is a Distortion. The statement in question compares monohulls to other ships, not jets.

(B) is another Distortion. The author is merely comparing monohulls to other ships, not drawing an analogy between them. The analogy in the argument is between monohulls and jets.

(C) is a 180. The distinction actually goes *against* the author's claim that monohulls will be profitable until the analogy overrules it.

(E) is a Distortion. The author's main conclusion is solely about monohulls. Comparing the ships' distinction to the planes' distinction is all part of the evidence. The statement in question also only discusses the relative transportation costs of each type of ship, but does not otherwise make distinctions about their characteristics.

21. (E) Strengthen

Step 1: Identify the Question Type

The question asks for something that will strengthen the given argument. Find an answer that validates the connection between the evidence and the conclusion.

Step 2: Untangle the Stimulus

The Keyword [*t*]*herefore* indicates the conclusion: maté probably originated in Paraguay. Why? Because maté is more varied and more widely used in Paraguay than anywhere else.

Step 3: Make a Prediction

The argument is all about maté. The evidence is about its varieties and usage, while the conclusion is about its origin.

The correct answer will validate the connection made by the author between those concepts—specifically that the place where maté is most varied and most widely used is most likely its place of origin.

Step 4: Evaluate the Answer Choices

(E) makes a helpful proportional connection between usage and origin. If a place uses something *more widely* as it's used for a *longer* time, then it stands to reason that the place with the *widest* usage (as is the case with maté in Paraguay) is likely to be where it's been used the *longest*, i.e., where it was first used.

(A) doesn't help in the same way as **(E)** because it doesn't give a proportional relationship. Even though variety may be an indication of how long something has been used, it still wouldn't necessarily mean Paraguay was the origin, even if it's been there a "very long time." For instance, even if there's a lack of variety in places where maté is relatively new, that doesn't mean the area with the *most* variety is the origin (where it's been around the longest). Maybe the origin country also lacks a lot of variety (e.g., uses only its purest variety).

(B) is a 180. This suggests that maté originated elsewhere and was brought to Paraguay as people migrated there.

(C) is Out of Scope. Even if Paraguayan people believe they have the *best* maté, that doesn't mean it originated there. After all, New Yorkers and Chicagoans often debate who has the best pizza, but it still originated in Italy.

(D) doesn't help. This just means maté is primarily consumed in South America, but it doesn't pinpoint Paraguay as the origin.

22. (A) Weaken (EXCEPT)

Step 1: Identify the Question Type

According to the question, a group of opponents are going to argue why family income has decreased. Four answers will counter, i.e., weaken their argument. The correct answer will be the exception—the one that strengthens or has no effect on the argument.

Step 2: Untangle the Stimulus

In a certain country, average family income decreased over an eight-year period. A political party's opponents argue that this decrease was caused by the party's economical mismanagement.

Step 3: Make a Prediction

The opponents provide no stated evidence, but they are concluding a causal relationship (economic mismanagement caused family income to drop). Such an argument would be weakened by indicating an alternate cause, e.g., another reason why average family income went down. Four answers will suggest alternate causes; the correct answer will not.

Step 4: Evaluate the Answer Choices

(A) is the exception. Even if family income went up in 1996, it still went down overall by 2004, and this answer does nothing to reject economic mismanagement as a cause for that decrease.

(B) weakens the argument directly by providing a "noneconomic" cause: fewer families with multiple incomes.

(C) weakens the argument by freeing the government of guilt and citing outside factors as the cause.

(D) weakens the argument by pointing to another noneconomic cause: the working population is getting younger, and younger people earn less money. No economic mismanagement there.

(E) directly weakens the opponents' claim by citing a *previous* party's policies as the cause for lower family incomes.

23. (A) Assumption (Necessary)

Step 1: Identify the Question Type

The question asks for what the argument "requires assuming," which means this is a Necessary Assumption question. Find the answer that must be true for the argument to work.

Step 2: Untangle the Stimulus

The author is comparing two groups of amateur gardeners. The first group chooses when to plant based on phases of the moon. The second group plants when the weather first gets warm in the spring. The author concludes (indicated by the Keyword [s]o) that the first group won't lose as many plants to frost. The evidence is that a frost can follow the first warm spell of spring.

Step 3: Make a Prediction

If the first warm spell of spring is followed by a frost, then plants from the second group of gardeners are certainly at risk. To better avoid frost damage, gardeners would have to wait a little longer before planting. The author must be assuming that gardeners using the moon phases must be doing this—waiting a little longer. That's the only way they'd be less at risk for frost damages.

Step 4: Evaluate the Answer Choices

(A) must be true. Using the Denial Test, if gardeners using moon phases planted at the *same time or earlier* than the other gardeners, they would be exposed to the exact same risk when a frost hits. The author must assume that they plant a little later in the season when there's less likely to be an unexpected frost.

(B) would certainly help the author's point: if phases of the moon affected frosts, then gardeners watching the phases could better predict a frost and avoid it. But despite its helpfulness, this isn't *required*, as the question demands. Even if the moon phases had *no* effect on frosts, they could still indicate a later planting time, helping gardeners avoid frost by happenstance.

(C) is an Irrelevant Comparison. Even if they all planted the *same* types of plants, the author's point could still be valid. Again, this *could* be helpful if the first group used frost-resistant plants and the second group didn't. However, that distinction isn't drawn here, and it still wouldn't *need* to be true.

(D) is Out of Scope. Whether gardeners understand what they're doing has no effect on the author's argument.

(E) is Out of Scope. The argument is about amateur gardeners, not professional ones. Nothing would need to be true about the pros for this argument to work.

24. (B) Inference

Step 1: Identify the Question Type

The correct answer will be "strongly supported" by the given information. That means it will be a deducible inference. Accept the given information as true, and combine whatever statements you can to make deductions.

Step 2: Untangle the Stimulus

The columnist is talking about the tourism industry in developing countries. On average, tourism companies owned by foreigners take in about 70 percent of tourism profits—a number that generally increases as a country becomes a popular tourist destination. This can be offset if tourists use locals for some services.

Step 3: Make a Prediction

Seventy percent is the *average* percentage going to foreign owners, which means there must be countries where the percentage is even *higher*. And those countries must be among the most popular if the percentage generally increases as popularity increases. The last line about tourists needs to be treated carefully. It merely says that tourists *can* counteract this situation. It doesn't say they *will*, and it doesn't say by how much. If the correct answer uses this information, it must retain the conservative language. Otherwise, the correct answer will merely be based on the facts from the first two sentences.

Step 4: Evaluate the Answer Choices

(B) is supported by the opening statistics. If the percentage of profits that goes to foreign owners increases with a country's popularity, then there must be *some* countries among the most popular that make above-average profits. And if the average is 70 percent, that's already well above *most* of the profits.

(A) is a Distortion. The author merely mentions that tourists *can* do this, but never comes out and suggests that they *should*.

(C) is possible, but not supported. If an average of 70 percent of tourism goes to foreigners, that means an average of 30 percent goes to locals. However, the countries where locals make an above-average percentage could still provide less than half of the services.

(D) is Extreme and a Distortion. Locals may get a smaller *percentage* of tourism profits, but they can still make more money if the total profits increase substantially. (For example, 25 percent of $20 million ($5 million) is still more than 30 percent of $10 million ($3 million).) Also, the profit figures deal only in tourism income. Even if the local people lose out on some of those revenues, nothing in the stimulus prevents them from possibly offsetting that loss by making more in a different industry. So, it is not supported that the locals will get "progressively poorer."

(E) is Extreme. Tourists who use local services can counteract foreign owners' profits to *some* degree, but they may still use foreign tourism business for some aspects of their vacation. It can't be said that they won't contribute "in any way" to foreign owners' profits.

25. (A) Assumption (Necessary)

Step 1: Identify the Question Type

The argument given "depends on assuming" the correct answer, which means this is a Necessary Assumption question.

Step 2: Untangle the Stimulus

The Keyword *therefore* indicates the conclusion: it's impossible to tell if the population of certain amphibians is being affected by industrial pollution. The evidence is that the population of most amphibians is affected by weather variations.

Step 3: Make a Prediction

If weather was a potential factor, then it would certainly be challenging to blame pollution. However, the argument's conclusion is about certain amphibian species identified by scientists in the first sentence. It's only said that *most* amphibians are affected by weather, not necessarily *all* amphibians—and certainly not necessarily the ones the scientists are talking about. In order for the argument to work properly, the author *must* assume that the amphibians cited are among those affected by the weather.

Step 4: Evaluate the Answer Choices

(A) is necessary for the author's argument. Be careful - interpreting all of the negatives. This basically says that the amphibians in question are not *un*affected by the weather (i.e., they *are* affected by weather).

(B) is a 180. To claim it's impossible to blame pollution, weather would have to have the *same* impact as pollution. Then it would be impossible to tell the difference. This says the exact opposite.

(C) isn't necessary. The author isn't saying it must be one or the other, exclusively. Even if the population could be affected by a combination of the two—or even an unmentioned third factor—the author can still validly claim that pollution is impossible to confirm.

(D) is a Distortion. This only relates how pollution can affect *certain* amphibians, but not necessarily the same amphibians in question in this argument.

(E) is Out of Scope. There's no distinction made as to whether the claimed pollution is severe or not, so it's impossible to apply the logic of this answer to the argument. Also, the answer can be eliminated using the Denial Test: if industrial pollution is severe, it *cannot* create more weather variations that would occur naturally. That fact wouldn't ruin the author's claim that it is impossible to determine what's causing the amphibian populations to decline.

Section IV: Logic Games

Game 1: Employee Bonuses

Q#	Question Type	Correct	Difficulty
1	Acceptability	C	★
2	"If" / Could Be True	B	★
3	"If" / Must Be True	A	★
4	Must Be True	E	★
5	"If" / Must Be True	D	★
6	Could Be True EXCEPT	B	★★

Game 2: Landscaper's Trees

Q#	Question Type	Correct	Difficulty
7	Acceptability	D	★
8	"If" / Must Be True	B	★
9	Complete and Accurate List	C	★★
10	"If" / Could Be True	A	★★★
11	Completely Determine	A	★★★

Game 3: Librarians' Desk Duty

Q#	Question Type	Correct	Difficulty
12	Acceptability	A	★
13	Must Be False (CANNOT Be True)	E	★
14	"If" / Must Be False (CANNOT Be True)	B	★
15	"If" / Must Be True	A	★★
16	"If" / Must Be True	C	★
17	"If" / Must Be True	D	★★
18	Rule Substitution	C	★★★

Game 4: Business Newsletter

Q#	Question Type	Correct	Difficulty
19	Acceptability	D	★★★
20	"If" / Must Be True	A	★★
21	Must Be False	E	★★★★
22	"If" / Must Be True	D	★★★
23	Could Be True EXCEPT	D	★★★

Game 1: Employee Bonuses

Step 1: Overview

Situation: An HR department giving out bonuses to employees

Entities: Seven employees—four in Finance (Kimura, Lopez, Meng, Peterson) and three in Graphics (Vaughan, Xavier, Zane); three bonus values ($1,000, $3,000, $5,000)

Action: Distribution. Determine the bonus for each employee. Each employee can only receive exactly one of the bonuses, which is why this is categorized as Distribution rather than Matching. However, the game could work conceptually as other actions, too. For instance, each bonus could be matched to a different employee, in which case, although each employee still receives exactly one bonus, each bonus could be repeated. Additionally, there is an argument for calling it a Sequencing game given that Rule 2 calls for some employees to be in a *larger* denomination group than some others. Remember, though, that however you classify a game is substantially less important than assuring you have a Master Sketch that allows you to build in rules and spot deductions.

Limitations: Each employee gets one bonus, but there's no limit to how many employees get each bonus.

Step 2: Sketch

List the employees by initial, using uppercase and lowercase letters to distinguish the two subgroups (Finance and Graphics). Set up a column for each bonus. The employees will be distributed once each.

FIN: K L M P
graph: v x z

$1 $3 $5

Note that the overview never states that each bonus value will be given out, so one or more columns may be blank. Therefore, don't add any slots in the columns until they've been established.

This sketch is consistent with a standard Distribution game, in which one set of entities is assigned once apiece to subgroups. However, some may find it unusual to assign people to bonuses—the real world usually works the other way around. That would suggest a sketch in which the seven people are listed on top, with one slot below each to assign the bonus. That type of setup would indicate a Matching game as noted as a possibility in Step 1.

$1 $3 $5
FIN   graph
K   L   M   P   v   x   z

In fact, the answers to the first question (an Acceptability question) use that setup. Ultimately, either sketch would work fine for this game, with no change in how deductions are made. These explanations will use the Distribution instead of the Matching configuration because a Distribution sketch would also be parallel to a Sequencing approach. However, neither the Distribution nor the Matching approach is superior. It is simply a matter of personal preference.

Step 3: Rules

Rule 1 sets a restriction on the three Graphics employees (Vaughan, Xavier, and Zane). None of them will receive a $1,000 bonus. Add "~v," "~x," and "~z" under the $1,000 column.

Rule 2 suggests that some people in each department may be rated Highly Effective. Within each department, those rated Highly Effective will make more than those not. Because the ratings haven't been assigned yet, draw a note to the side that expresses the rule: "Each dept: Not High Eff $ < High Eff $."

Rule 3 rates all of the employees. Lopez, Meng, and Xavier are Highly Effective. The rest are not. Mark L, M, and x (e.g., star them, circle them, or underline them) to indicate this rating.

Step 4: Deductions

There's not much to work with, but there's enough to make some serious deductions. Start with the Finance Department. Two of them (Lopez and Meng) are Highly Effective; the others (Kimura and Peterson) are not. That means Lopez and Meng must get bigger bonuses than Kimura and Peterson.

K & P < L & M

That means Lopez and Meng cannot get $1,000 bonuses, and Kimura and Peterson cannot get $5,000 bonuses. Note that neither pair has to receive the same bonuses. In other words, Lopez and Meng can get different bonuses, as long as both of their bonuses are greater than Kimura's and Peterson's.

There are a few ways the Finance bonuses can work out. However, it's helpful to note that if one Finance person gets a $3,000 bonus, that will be significant. For example, if Kimura receives a $3,000 bonus, then Lopez and Meng must both get $5,000 bonuses. Peterson could then get either $1,000 or $3,000. Don't worry about considering every outcome, but do take note of the limited ways these bonuses can be paid out.

The Graphics department provides even bigger deductions. There, Xavier is Highly Effective, while Vaughan and Zane are not. So, Xavier gets the biggest bonus. However, none of the Graphics employees get a $1,000 bonus (Rule 1). That can only mean Vaughan and Zane get $3,000 bonuses and Xavier gets $5,000.

One final note: Even though Meng and Lopez are Highly Effective while Vaughan and Zane are not, Meng and Lopez do not necessarily have to receive bigger bonuses than Vaughan and Zane. Rule 2 only applies to employees *in the same department*.

A Master Sketch of this game—set up as a Distribution game—would look something like this:

FIN: K L̇ Ṁ P   * = high eff

graph: v ẋ z   not high eff < high eff

$1	$3	$5
	v	x
	z	

K & P < L & M

~L   ~K
~M   ~P

Step 5: Questions

1. (C) Acceptability

As with all Acceptability questions, the four wrong answers will each violate one or more rules. Use the rules to find the violators and eliminate them. While the first rule is easily tested here, the second and third rules will need to be tested together.

(B) and **(E)** violate Rule 1 by giving $1,000 bonuses to a Graphics employee. **(A)** violates Rule 2 by giving Highly Effective employee Xavier (Rule 3) the same bonus as everyone else in the Graphics department. **(D)** violates Rule 2 by giving Highly Effective employee Meng (Rule 3) the same bonus as co-Finance employee Kimura, who is *not* Highly Effective. That leaves **(C)** as the correct answer.

2. (B) "If" / Could Be True

For this question, Lopez and Meng receive different bonuses. As Highly Effective employees, they cannot get $1,000 bonuses, so one must get $3,000 and the other $5,000. The non-Highly Effective Finance employees (Kimura and Peterson) can now only get $1,000 bonuses.

$1	$3	$5
K	v	x
P	z	M/L
	L/M	

Lopez could get a $3,000 bonus, making **(B)** the correct answer. All four of the other answers must be false.

3. (A) "If" / Must Be True

For this question, only one person gets a $1,000 bonus. It cannot be a Graphics employee (Rule 1), so it must be a Finance employee—and it cannot be a Highly Effective employee (Rule 2). That means either Kimura or Peterson gets the $1,000 bonus. The other must receive a $3,000 bonus so that Meng and Lopez (the Highly Effective Finance employees) can get bigger bonuses: $5,000 each.

$1	$3	$5
K/P	v	x
	z	M
	P/K	L

Meng has to get a $5,000 bonus, making **(A)** the correct answer. **(B)**, **(D)**, and **(E)** all could be true, but need not be, and **(C)** must be false.

4. (E) Must Be True

The correct answer to this question must be true, which means the four wrong answers could be false.

None of the Graphics employees get a $1,000 bonus, and it's possible for Kimura and Peterson to get $3,000 bonuses with Meng and Lopez getting $5,000 bonuses. Nobody needs to get a $1,000 bonus, which eliminates **(A)**.

Two employees (Vaughan and Zane) already receive $3,000 bonuses. However, nobody else needs to. It's possible for Kimura and Peterson to get $1,000 bonuses while Meng and Lopez get $5,000 bonuses. That eliminates **(B)**.

Still, it *is* possible for Kimura and Peterson to both get $3,000 bonuses, which makes it possible that *four* employees get $3,000 bonuses. So, there could be more than three such employees, eliminating **(C)**.

Xavier definitely gets a $5,000 bonus. However, nobody else needs to. It's possible that Kimura and Peterson get $1,000 bonuses while Lopez and Meng get $3,000 bonuses. That eliminates **(D)**.

Because there are Highly Effective employees in each department, only those employees can get $5,000 bonuses. There are only three such employees (Rule 3), so that confirms **(E)** as the correct answer.

5. (D) "If" / Must Be True

For this question, only two employees get a $5,000 bonus. One of them is Xavier. The other must come from the Finance department. It must be a Highly Effective Finance employee, so it must be Lopez or Meng. The other one still has to make more than Kimura and Peterson, so the other will receive a $3,000 bonus with Kimura and Peterson receiving $1,000 bonuses.

$1	$3	$5
K	v	x
P	z	M/L
	L/M	

Peterson gets a $1,000 bonus, making **(D)** the correct answer. **(A)**, **(B)**, and **(C)** could be false, and **(E)** must be false.

6. (B) Could Be True EXCEPT

The four wrong answers here all could be true. The correct answer will be the one that must be false.

Two employees (Vaughan and Zane) already receive $3,000 bonuses. There could also be exactly two employees who receive $1,000 bonuses (Kimura and Peterson).

$1	$3	$5
K	V	X
P	Z	L
		M

(A) is possible, so that can be eliminated.

However, Kimura and Peterson are the only employees who even *can* receive $1,000 bonuses. Therefore, the number of employees who get $1,000 bonuses can never exceed the number who get $3,000 bonuses because there will always be at least two in the $3,000 bonus category—Vaughan and Zane. That makes **(B)** impossible, and thus the correct answer. For the record:

The mini-sketch for the previous question shows that both **(C)** and **(E)** are possible. Kimura and Peterson can get $1,000 bonuses while Xavier, along with exactly one of Meng or Lopez, can get $5,000 bonuses. **(D)** is possible if Kimura and Peterson get $1,000 bonuses, and Xavier is the only employee to get a $5,000 bonus.

$1	$3	$5
K	V	X
P	Z	
	L	
	M	

Game 2: Landscaper's Trees

Step 1: Overview

Situation: A landscaper planting trees in three lots

Entities: Seven trees (hickory, larch, maple, oak, plum, sycamore, walnut); three lots (1, 2, 3)

Action: Distribution. Determine in which lot each tree is planted. Each tree must be planted somewhere, but no tree can be planted in more than one lot. That's why this is a Distribution game rather than a Matching game.

Limitations: There are exactly seven trees, and each tree must be planted. There is no limit to how many trees can be planted in each lot. At this juncture, a lot could receive anywhere from zero to seven trees.

Step 2: Sketch

A standard Distribution sketch will do. List the trees by initial, and set up columns for the three lots. Because the overview sets no numbers on the lots, do not add slots to the columns until rules or deductions dictate.

H L M O P S W

1   2   3

Step 3: Rules

Rule 1 sets the makeup for one of the lots: hickory, oak, and *exactly* one other. This could be any of the three lots, so draw this Block of Entities to the side, including a single blank space to be filled in later.

H
O
—

Rule 2 prevents maple and walnut from being together.

M̸
W̸

Rule 3 establishes at least one tree on lot 1: larch or walnut. However, larch and walnut cannot be planted together. So, add "L/W" under lot 1. Additionally, depending on which type of notation you find more helpful, either make a note about the restriction ("Never LW") or add W/L to your sketch with arrows pointing to lots 2 and 3.

Rule 4 establishes at least one tree on lot 2: maple or oak. And they cannot be together. So again, add "M/O" under column 2 and, depending on which type of notation you find more helpful, either note the restriction ("Never MO") or add O/M to your sketch with arrows pointing to lots 1 and 3.

Rule 5 adds a numeric restriction: lot 3 has to include more trees than lot 1.

Step 4: Deductions

Rule 1 presents a significant Block of Entities consisting of three trees. That block is restricted by the last rule. It can no longer be placed on lot 1. After all, if there were three trees on lot 1, there would have to be at least four trees on lot 3. That would be all seven trees, leaving nothing for lot 2 and thus violating Rule 4.

Therefore, the block from Rule 1 can only be placed on lot 2 or lot 3. This is a great opportunity for Limited Options.

In the first option, the block with hickory, oak, and one other will be placed on lot 2. That leaves four trees to be planted in the remaining lots. The only way to make sure lot 3 gets more trees than lot 1 is to place three trees on lot 3 and one on lot 1. The one tree on lot 1 will be larch or walnut (Rule 3).

Maple cannot be on lot 2 with oak (Rule 4). With no more room on lot 1, maple must be placed on lot 3.

I)	1	2	3
	L/W	H	M
		O	—

In the second option, the block with hickory, oak, and one other will be placed on lot 3. That leaves four trees to be planted in the remaining lots. Lots 1 and 2 each have at least one tree, but lot 1 cannot get three (Rule 5). So, lot 1 gets only one or two trees, with lot 2 getting three or two trees. That means lot 2 gets at least a second tree, so add a slot to that column. Furthermore, with oak on lot 3, maple must be one of the trees on lot 2 (Rule 4).

II)	1	2	3
	L/W	M	H
		—	O

Note: These options could also be derived by using Rule 4. Maple and oak are both duplicated in the rules, making it significant which one is placed on lot 2. Each option would automatically place the block from Rule 1, leading to the exact same set of options.

Also note that plum and sycamore are never mentioned in the rules. They are Floaters and can be placed anywhere there's an empty space. Make a notation, such as starring them, in your Master Sketch. Because there are two Floaters, they are entirely interchangeable.

The final Master Sketch will look something like this:

H L M O P S̃ W

I)

	1	2	3
	L/W	H	M
		O	

M̶ L̶ M̶
W̶ W̶ O̶

II)

	1	2	3	1 < 3
	L/W	M	H
			O

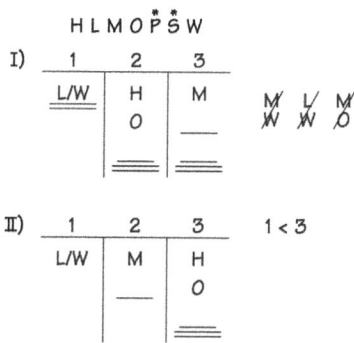

Step 5: Questions

7. (D) Acceptability

As with any Acceptability question, go through the rules one at a time, eliminating answers that violate those rules.

(A) violates Rule 1 by placing hickory and oak on lot 2 with nothing else. None of the answers violate Rule 2. **(C)** violates Rule 3 by not having larch or walnut on lot 1. **(E)** violates Rule 4 by not placing maple or oak on lot 2. **(B)** violates Rule 5 by putting the same number of trees on lots 1 and 3. That leaves **(D)** as the correct answer.

8. (B) "If" / Must Be True

For this question, hickory will be on lot 2. This is the basis for the first Limited Option. In that option, lot 3 must include maple, making **(B)** the correct answer.

9. (C) Complete and Accurate List

The correct answer to this question will list every tree that could possibly be planted on lot 1—not necessarily all at once though. The four wrong answers will list trees that *cannot* ever be on lot 1 or leave out trees that *could* be.

By Rule 5, lot 1 cannot include the three-tree block with hickory and oak. Otherwise, there would have to be four trees on lot 3, leaving nothing for lot 2, thus violating Rule 4. So, hickory cannot be on lot 1. That eliminates **(A)** and **(B)**.

By Rule 3, lot 1 must contain larch or walnut. Either one is acceptable, so that eliminates **(E)**, which does not list larch.

The only difference between **(C)** and **(D)** is that **(C)** lists sycamore. Because both plum and sycamore are Floaters, they're interchangeable. There'd be no reason one could be on lot 1 and the other could not. Therefore, if there were a second tree planted on lot 1, it could be either plum or sycamore. That eliminates **(D)**, which is missing sycamore.

That leaves **(C)** as the correct answer. To save time, it would have been very effective to skip this question temporarily and work on the next one first. In the next question, the sketch places the larch on lot 1, and the correct answer places the sycamore on lot 1. That means the correct answer to this

question would have to include those two trees, and **(C)** is the only one to do so.

10. (A) "If" / Could Be True

For this question, walnut is planted on lot 3. This could only happen in the second option because in the first option maple is established on lot 3, and maple and walnut cannot be together by Rule 2. So, using the second option, walnut would fill up lot 3. Larch would have to be planted on lot 1 (Rule 3). The remaining trees—the two Floaters (plum and sycamore)—can both go on lot 2, or they can be split so that one goes on lot 1 and the other goes on lot 2.

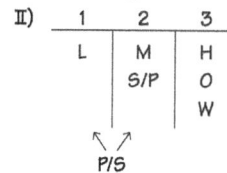

II)

	1	2	3
	L	M	H
		S/P	O
			W

↖ ↗
P/S

The sycamore could be planted on lot 1, making **(A)** the correct answer.

This question could still be successfully approached even without the Limited Options. Placing walnut on lot 3 would still force larch to lot 1 (Rule 3). Maple couldn't be on lot 3 with walnut (Rule 2). It also couldn't be on lot 1 with the larch because that would place at least three trees on lot 3 (Rule 5), leaving only two trees for lot 2. The block with oak from Rule 1 would have to be placed on lot 3, but then lot 2 would be without maple or oak, violating Rule 4. So, the maple must be on lot 2.

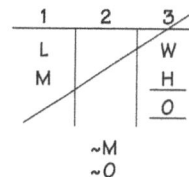

	1	2	3
	L		W
	M		H
			O

~M
~O

At that point, the oak couldn't be on lot 2 (Rule 2). To satisfy numbers, the block with the oak can only be placed on lot 3. So, that lot will include hickory, oak, and walnut, and that's it. Plum and sycamore would be placed either one each on lots 1 and 2 or both on lot 2.

11. (A) Completely Determine

The correct answer to this question will be a tree that, when planted on lot 2, will make it possible to determine exactly where every other tree is planted with no uncertainty.

If the walnut is on lot 2, then the larch would have to be on lot 1 (Rule 3). The maple couldn't be on lot 2 (Rule 2), so the oak would have to be (Rule 4). Lot 2 would have to include hickory and one other tree (Rule 1)—in this case, the walnut. Lot 2 would then be filled. To satisfy Rule 5, the remaining four trees would have to be split one onto lot 1 and three onto lot 3. Lot 1 is already done with larch, so the remaining trees (maple, plum, and sycamore) will round out lot 3.

1	2	3
L	W	M
	O	P
	H	S

So, planting walnut on lot 2 would lead to just one possible outcome, making **(A)** the correct answer. For the record:

Plum and sycamore are Floaters. Either one could be placed on lot 2 with maple or oak. Because there would be multiple outcomes in either case, that eliminates **(B)** and **(C)**.

Placing the maple on lot 2 would force out oak. By the numbers of Rule 5, the block with oak (including hickory and one other) would be forced onto lot 3. However, lot 1 could still have either larch or walnut, and plum and sycamore could be planted anywhere.

1	2	3
L/W	M	H
		O
		—

~W

With too many possibilities, that eliminates **(D)**.

If larch is on lot 2, then walnut would be on lot 1 (Rule 3). However, lot 2 could contain either maple or oak, so there are still multiple outcomes.

1	2	3
W	L	
	M/O	

That eliminates **(E)**.

KAPLAN

Game 3: Librarians' Desk Duty

Step 1: Overview

Situation: Librarians being scheduled for desk duty

Entities: Seven librarians (Flynn, Gomez, Hill, Kitson, Leung, Moore, Zahn)

Action: Loose Sequencing. Determine the order in which the librarians are scheduled for desk duty, from Monday to Saturday. A look ahead at the rules shows that every rule involves relative ordering (i.e., one person is on duty at some undefined point *earlier* than another). That makes it Loose Sequencing—even though there will be one "tie" in the sequence for the two librarians on Saturday.

Limitations: There are seven librarians, but only six days. One librarian will be on duty every weekday, Monday through Friday. Two will be on duty on the last day, Saturday. Every librarian will be on duty exactly once.

Step 2: Sketch

As with any Sequencing game, simply list the entities by initial. Because it's Loose Sequencing, the final diagram is likely to be a tree, so drawing a series of slots is not necessary. However, if you also drew out seven slots, that's fine given the brief nature of the task. The slots can be a helpful visual reminder for remembering the double duty of Saturday, but the rules themselves do not allow entities to be built into definite slots of a Strict Sequencing sketch.

F G H K L M Z

Mo	Tu	We	Th	Fr	Sa
—	—	—	—	—	—

—

Step 3: Rules

Rule 1 provides a simple relationship: Hill is on duty before Leung.

H — L

Rule 2 sets up a relationship among three librarians: Hill and Moore are on duty before Gomez. Note that no relationship is defined between Hill and Moore, so they could be scheduled in either order. You can add this rule directly to the sketch from Rule 1.

$$H \diagdown \begin{matrix} L \\ \diagdown G \\ M \diagup \end{matrix}$$

Rule 3 provides more connections. Flynn is on duty before Kitson and Moore, but the relationship between Kitson and Moore is undefined. That information can all be attached to the evolving sketch.

$$\begin{matrix} & & L \\ H & \diagdown & \diagdown G \\ & & M \diagup \\ F & \diagup & \diagdown K \end{matrix}$$

Rule 4 is a final simple relationship: Kitson is on duty before Zahn. Add that to the Loose Sequencing sketch.

$$\begin{matrix} & & L \\ H & \diagdown & \diagdown G \\ & & M \diagup \\ F & \diagup & \diagdown K — Z \end{matrix}$$

Rule 5 states that Leung must be on duty before Flynn, with one exception: when Leung is scheduled for Saturday. The Formal Logic of this rule is technically set up as follows:

$$\sim(L...F) \rightarrow \frac{Sa}{L}$$

$$\frac{\sim Sa}{L} \rightarrow L...F$$

However, rather than jotting the Formal Logic down, the rule can be used to make a deduction as discussed in Step 4 next.

Step 4: Deductions

The last rule sets up two possible outcomes. The first is when Leung is scheduled for Saturday. In that case, Leung is simply one of two Saturday librarians, and the rule provides no further restrictions. Per the rule, Flynn could be earlier than Leung or could be scheduled simultaneously with Leung on Saturday (although Rule 3 already prohibits Flynn from performing on Saturday). The second is when Leung is scheduled for any other day. In that case, Leung must be on duty before Flynn. These should be drawn out as Limited Options.

The first option involves Leung being scheduled for Saturday. In that case, nothing else is deduced. Simply mark L as "Sa" (or add L under Saturday if a sketch with slots is used).

$$I) \quad \begin{matrix} & & \frac{Sa}{L} \\ & H & \diagdown \\ & & \diagdown G \\ & & M \diagup \\ F & \diagup & \diagdown K — Z \end{matrix}$$

In the second option, Leung must be placed before Flynn. This leads to some bigger deductions. Flynn will be preceded by Leung, who in turn still needs to be preceded by Hill (Rule 1). Flynn must still be placed before Moore (Rule 3), who must be placed before Gomez (Rule 2). That puts five librarians in order. The last two librarians are Kitson, who is still scheduled after Flynn (Rule 3), and Zahn, who is still scheduled after Kitson (Rule 4).

With everyone in order, the first three librarians in the schedule must be Hill, Leung, and Flynn, in that order. So, they will be on Monday, Tuesday, and Wednesday. The remaining four librarians will be scheduled after Flynn on the last three days.

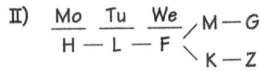

$$
\text{II)} \quad \underline{\text{Mo}} \;\; \underline{\text{Tu}} \;\; \underline{\text{We}} \begin{array}{c} \diagup \; \text{M} - \text{G} \\ \text{H} - \text{L} - \text{F} \\ \diagdown \; \text{K} - \text{Z} \end{array}
$$

Step 5: Questions

12. (A) Acceptability

The correct answer here will be acceptable—the one answer that doesn't violate any rules. Go through the rules one at a time and eliminate the four answers that violate those rules.

(E) violates Rule 1 by scheduling Hill *later* than Leung. No answer violates Rule 2. **(C)** violates Rule 3 by scheduling Flynn *later* than Kitson and Moore. **(D)** violates Rule 4 by scheduling Kitson *later* than Zahn. **(B)** violates Rule 5 because Leung is not on Saturday, which means Leung should be scheduled *earlier* than Flynn, not *later*. That leaves **(A)** as the correct answer, which is acceptable because Leung is scheduled for Saturday, negating the need for Leung to be scheduled before Flynn.

13. (E) Must Be False (CANNOT Be True)

The correct answer to this question will be a librarian that *cannot* be on duty on Tuesday. The remaining four will be librarians that *could* be on duty on Tuesday.

If Leung is on duty on Saturday, then Flynn doesn't have to be preceded by anyone. The same is true of Hill. So, either Flynn or Hill could be on duty on Monday, allowing the other to be on duty on Tuesday. That eliminates **(A)** and **(B)**.

Kitson merely has to be on duty after Flynn. If Flynn was on duty on Monday, then Kitson could be scheduled on Tuesday. That eliminates **(C)**. This is also the case for Moore, which eliminates **(D)**.

Zahn has to be on duty after Kitson (Rule 4), who in turn has to be on duty after Flynn (Rule 3). That means Zahn will always have at least two librarians scheduled ahead of him. So, he couldn't possibly be on duty earlier than Wednesday. With Tuesday an impossibility, **(E)** is the correct answer.

14. (B) "If" / Must Be False (CANNOT Be True)

For this question, Kitson will be on duty before Moore. This could happen in either option, so consider the general implications. Kitson still needs to be on duty after Flynn (Rule 3), and Moore still needs to be on duty before Gomez (Rule 2).

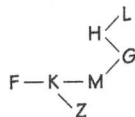

$$
\text{F} - \text{K} - \text{M} \begin{array}{c} \diagup \; \text{H} \diagdown \text{L} \\ \diagdown \text{G} \\ \diagdown \text{Z} \end{array}
$$

The question is asking for something that *cannot* be true. In this case, Kitson must be on duty earlier than Gomez. It cannot be the other way around, making **(B)** the correct answer. **(A)**, **(C)**, **(D)**, and **(E)** all could be true.

15. (A) "If" / Must Be True

For this question, Zahn must be on duty on Thursday. This cannot happen in the second option because Zahn needs to be scheduled after too many people (Hill, Leung, Flynn, and Kitson). Therefore, if Zahn is on duty on Thursday, it can only occur in the first option. In that option, Leung must be on duty on Saturday. Flynn couldn't possibly be on duty on Saturday, so Flynn must be on duty earlier than Leung, making **(A)** the correct answer.

This can be seen without Limited Options as well. If Zahn is on Thursday, Kitson must be on duty earlier (Rule 4), which means Flynn must as well (Rule 3).

That leaves one more space in the schedule before Zahn. Leung couldn't be on duty before Zahn without also scheduling Hill earlier (Rule 1). Likewise, Gomez couldn't be on duty before Zahn without also scheduling Moore earlier (Rule 2). Therefore, Leung and Gomez have to be scheduled *later* than Zahn. One of Hill and Moore will be scheduled before Zahn and one after. Regardless of everyone's exact positions, Flynn is guaranteed to be before Leung. **(B)**, **(C)**, **(D)**, and **(E)** all could be false.

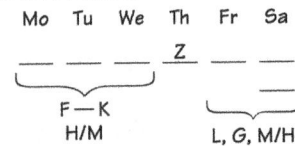

$$
\begin{array}{cccccc}
\text{Mo} & \text{Tu} & \text{We} & \text{Th} & \text{Fr} & \text{Sa} \\
\underline{} & \underline{} & \underline{} & \underline{\text{Z}} & \underline{} & \underline{} \\
\end{array}
$$

$$
\underbrace{}_{\substack{\text{F} - \text{K} \\ \text{H/M}}} \qquad \underbrace{}_{\text{L, G, M/H}}
$$

16. (C) "If" / Must Be True

For this question, Moore will be on duty on Tuesday. That can only happen in the first option (in the second option, Leung is on Tuesday). In the first option, with Moore on Tuesday, Flynn—before Moore per Rule 3—must be on duty on Monday. The only other entity that is guaranteed a specific date for desk duty in the first option is Leung on Saturday. That makes **(C)** the correct answer.

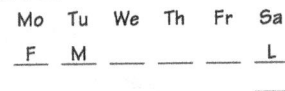

$$
\begin{array}{cccccc}
\text{Mo} & \text{Tu} & \text{We} & \text{Th} & \text{Fr} & \text{Sa} \\
\underline{\text{F}} & \underline{\text{M}} & \underline{} & \underline{} & \underline{} & \underline{\text{L}} \\
\end{array}
$$

Even without the Limited Options, it is known that Moore on Tuesday means Flynn on Monday (Rule 3). And, because Flynn is first, she'll automatically be on duty before Leung, which can only happen with Leung scheduled on Saturday (Rule 5). Answers about Thursday—**(A)** and **(B)**—or about Zahn—**(D)** and **(E)**—are all incorrect because they could be false.

17. (D) "If" / Must Be True

For this question, Flynn will be on duty earlier than Hill, which automatically points to the second option because in the first option Hill is before Flynn. In the second option, the new-"if" schedules Flynn before Hill, who must be on duty earlier than Leung (Rule 1). That means Flynn will be scheduled before

Leung, which means Leung must be scheduled on Saturday (Rule 5).

```
              Sa
        ┌ H — L
    F ─┼── M — G
        └ K — Z
```

The only librarians who can also be scheduled on Saturday are Gomez and Kitson—the only other librarians who do not have to be scheduled earlier than someone else. So, every other librarian, including Moore, must be scheduled earlier than Leung. That means **(D)** must be true. **(A)**, **(B)**, **(C)**, and **(E)** all provide relationships that could be false.

18. (C) Rule Substitution

This question removes Rule 3 from the game and asks for a substitution that doesn't change any of the game's restrictions. In other words, the correct answer will be a rule that does exactly what the original Rule 3 did without adding any new restrictions. So, the correct answer must ensure Flynn's position before Kitson and Moore.

Restricting Flynn from Thursday does nothing to place Flynn before or after Kitson and Moore. This rule would allow Flynn to be on Friday or Saturday, which was never allowed by the original rule. That eliminates **(A)**.

By the original rules, Flynn and Hill were indeed the only librarians who could be on duty on Monday. However, this rule only works if Flynn were on duty on Monday. If Hill were on duty, this rule does nothing to connect Flynn with Kitson and Moore. That eliminates **(B)**.

If Hill and Leung are the only librarians that can be on duty before Flynn, then Flynn would have to be on duty before everyone else, including Kitson and Moore. This rule would also force Flynn to be on duty before Gomez and Zahn, but that was always true anyway because Moore is on duty before Gomez (Rule 2), and Kitson is on duty before Zahn (Rule 4). So, Rule 3 is back in effect, and there are no new restrictions. That makes **(C)** the correct answer. For the record:

Having Flynn on duty before Gomez does not necessarily place Flynn on duty before Moore. That eliminates **(D)**.

Having Flynn on duty before Zahn does not necessarily place Flynn on duty before Kitson. That eliminates **(E)**.

Game 4: Business Newsletter

Step 1: Overview

Situation: Setting up an issue of a business newsletter

Entities: Five slots (numbered 1 through 5); four feature types (finance, industry, marketing, technology) and one non-feature type (graphic)

Action: Matching. Determine in which slots the features will be assigned. What makes this game difficult to classify is that it doesn't fit the standard model of any one game type. It appears to have Strict Sequencing elements (the slots are described as "consecutive" in the first rule) and even Selection elements (some features may not be included). However, the rules and questions focus primarily on Matching concepts: assigning features—which can be repeated—to various slots. Whatever the label, the sketch shouldn't change, and the rules will be interpreted the same. Those factors are more important to managing the game than fixating on what the exact label should be.

Limitations: There are five slots and four feature types, as well as a non-feature type (graphic). Three features must be included, but there could be more. It's possible that some feature types will go unused, and there's no indication that feature types can only be used once. So, for example, it's possible that the three features are all finance. The game is very open-ended, made even more so by the first rule, which suggests that features can be spread out over multiple slots.

Step 2: Sketch

The sketch may be the most standard aspect of the game. There should be five slots numbered 1 through 5. Those slots will be filled with the entities, which should be listed by initial—including four uppercase letters for the features and one lowercase "g" for the non-feature graphic.

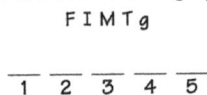

$$F\ I\ M\ T\ g$$

$$\overline{\underset{1}{\quad}}\ \overline{\underset{2}{\quad}}\ \overline{\underset{3}{\quad}}\ \overline{\underset{4}{\quad}}\ \overline{\underset{5}{\quad}}$$

Step 3: Rules

Rule 1 introduces the idea of features taking up multiple slots. If that happens, the slots must be next to one another. Make a shorthand of this to the side (e.g., "multi-slot features consecutive"). There are two things to note: First, if one feature does take up two slots, it's still considered *one* feature. To satisfy the requirement from the overview, there would still need to be at least two more features. Second, this only applies to single multi-slot features. It does not apply if there are two separate features of the same type. So, for example, one finance feature that takes up two slots would have to be in consecutive slots (e.g., 2 and 3). However, two *separate* finance features could be split up (e.g., slots 2 and 5).

Rule 2 is conditional. If there are any finance or technology features included, one of them must be in slot 1. By contrapositive, if slot 1 has neither finance nor technology, then there can be no finance or technology features at all in the issue.

$$F\ or\ T \rightarrow \frac{F/T}{1}$$

$$\frac{\sim F/T}{1} \rightarrow\ \sim F\ \&\ \sim T$$

Note: If there are no finance or technology features, then there's no restriction to the first slot.

Rule 3 limits the number of industry features to one. There doesn't *have* to be one, but there can't be more.

$$1\ I\ feature\ MAX$$

Step 4: Deductions

This game is way too open-ended to allow for deductions. There are no Blocks of Entities. There are no Established Entities. No entities are Duplicated in the rules. Numbers are important, but there can be anywhere from three to five features, and those features can be placed in single slots or spread out among multiple slots. And everything (except for industry) can be repeated as needed. This game will be all about understanding the rules and their implications.

Step 5: Questions

19. (D) Acceptability

As with typical Acceptability questions, go through the rules one at a time, eliminating answers that violate those rules.

(E) violates Rule 1 by splitting up a single marketing feature into two nonconsecutive slots. **(B)** violates Rule 2 by placing a graphic in slot 1 when there are technology features listed in the issue. **(C)** also violates Rule 2 by placing an industry feature in slot 1 when there's a finance feature listed in the issue. **(A)** violates Rule 3 by listing two industry features. That leaves **(D)** as the correct answer. (Note that even though this choice lists an industry feature in two slots, it's still listed as a single feature. So, this does not violate Rule 3.)

20. (A) "If" / Must Be True

For this question, there are no technology features but at least one finance feature. By Rule 2, that means slot 1 must include a finance feature.

$$\frac{F}{1}\ \overline{\underset{2}{\quad}}\ \overline{\underset{3}{\quad}}\ \boxed{\frac{F}{4}\ \overline{\underset{5}{\quad}}}$$

That makes **(A)** the correct answer. This question merely tests an understanding of Rule 2.

21. (E) Must Be False

The correct answer to this question must be impossible. The four wrong answers will all be possible, if not definitely true.

There could be a single industry feature in slot 1, as long as there were no finance or technology features in the issue. That eliminates **(A)**.

With a finance feature included, slot 1 would have to be a finance or technology feature (Rule 2). If slot 2 had the *only* finance feature, then slot 1 could still have technology. This is acceptable, which eliminates **(B)**.

Similarly, with a technology feature included, slot 1 would have to be finance or technology. If slot 3 had the *only* technology feature, slot 1 could still have finance. This is acceptable, which eliminates **(C)**.

If slot 1 had a feature that wasn't finance or marketing, it would have to be technology or industry. Filling slot 1 with a technology feature would ensure Rule 2 isn't violated. This is acceptable, which eliminates **(D)**.

If slot 5 had a feature—not a graphic—that wasn't industry or marketing, it would have to be finance or technology. However, by Rule 2, that would mean there would also have to be a finance or technology feature in slot 1. That would mean another feature that's *not* industry or marketing, making **(E)** impossible and thus the correct answer.

22. (D) "If" / Must Be True

For this question, there will be one industry feature and it will be in slot 1. According to the overview, there need to be at least two more features. With slot 1 occupied by an industry feature, the issue can no longer contain any finance or technology features (Rule 2). And there cannot be any more industry features (Rule 3). So, to fulfill the feature quota, there must be at least two marketing features. However, they can occupy any of the remaining four slots.

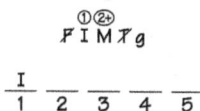

$$\cancel{F} \;\; I \;\; M \;\; \cancel{T} \;\; g$$

$$\frac{I}{1} \;\; \frac{}{2} \;\; \frac{}{3} \;\; \frac{}{4} \;\; \frac{}{5}$$

The industry feature may be spread over multiple slots, but it certainly doesn't have to be. That eliminates **(A)** and **(B)**.

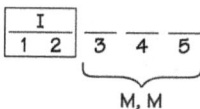

The marketing features could be assigned to slots 4 and 5, so they don't have to be assigned to either slot 2 or 3. That eliminates **(C)**.

$$\frac{I}{1} \;\; \frac{}{2} \;\; \frac{}{3} \;\; \frac{M}{4} \;\; \frac{M}{5}$$

There must be at least two marketing features, and slot 1 is already taken up by an industry feature. Even if one marketing feature was assigned to slot 5, the other one would *still* have to be assigned to slot 2, 3, or 4. There's no way to avoid putting at least one marketing feature in those slots.

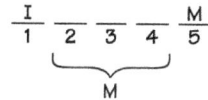

$$\frac{I}{1} \;\; \frac{}{2} \;\; \frac{}{3} \;\; \frac{}{4} \;\; \frac{M}{5}$$

(D) must happen, making it the correct answer. For the record:

The marketing features could be assigned to slots 2 and 4, so they don't have to be assigned to either slot 3 or 5—those slots could be graphics.

$$\frac{I}{1} \;\; \frac{M}{2} \;\; \frac{g}{3} \;\; \frac{M}{4} \;\; \frac{g}{5}$$

Even though slots 2 and 4 are not consecutive, this does not violate Rule 1. Remember, that rule only applies to a single multi-slot feature. Two separate marketing features can still be split up.

23. (D) Could Be True EXCEPT

Four answers to this question will be possible. The correct answer will be the exception—the one that must be false no matter what. For each answer, it's important to remember that each issue must include at least three features (according to the overview).

With only one finance feature, the issue still needs at least two more features. If there are no industry or marketing features, the other features would be technology ones. That is acceptable, which eliminates **(A)**.

With only one industry feature, the issue still needs at least two more features. If there are no finance or marketing features, the other features would be technology ones. That is acceptable, which eliminates **(B)**.

With only one finance feature, the issue still needs at least two more features. If there are no marketing or technology features, the other features would be finance ones. That is acceptable, which eliminates **(C)**.

With only one marketing feature, the issue still needs at least two more features. If there are no finance or technology features, the other features would be industry ones. However, there cannot be more than one industry feature. This is not acceptable, making **(D)** the correct answer. This question merely tests knowledge of the numbers limitation from the overview along with Rule 3. For the record:

With only one marketing feature, the issue still needs at least two more features. If there are no industry or technology features, the other features would be finance ones. That is acceptable, which eliminates **(E)**.

Glossary

Logical Reasoning

Logical Reasoning Question Types

Argument-Based Questions

Main Point Question

A question that asks for an argument's conclusion or an author's main point. Typical question stems:

Which one the following most accurately expresses the conclusion of the argument as a whole?

Which one of the following sentences best expresses the main point of the scientist's argument?

Role of a Statement Question

A question that asks how a specific sentence, statement, or idea functions within an argument. Typical question stems:

Which one of the following most accurately describes the role played in the argument by the statement that automation within the steel industry allowed steel mills to produce more steel with fewer workers?

The claim that governmental transparency is a nation's primary defense against public-sector corruption figures in the argument in which one of the following ways?

Point at Issue Question

A question that asks you to identify the specific claim, statement, or recommendation about which two speakers/authors disagree (or, rarely, about which they agree). Typical question stems:

A point at issue between Tom and Jerry is

The dialogue most strongly supports the claim that Marilyn and Billy disagree with each other about which one of the following?

Method of Argument Question

A question that asks you to describe an author's argumentative strategy. In other words, the correct answer describes *how* the author argues (not necessarily what the author says). Typical question stems:

Which one of the following most accurately describes the technique of reasoning employed by the argument?

Julian's argument proceeds by

In the dialogue, Alexander responds to Abigail in which one of the following ways?

Parallel Reasoning Question

A question that asks you to identify the answer choice containing an argument that has the same logical structure and reaches the same type of conclusion as the argument in the stimulus does. Typical question stems:

The pattern of reasoning in which one of the following arguments is most parallel to that in the argument above?

The pattern of reasoning in which one of the following arguments is most similar to the pattern of reasoning in the argument above?

Assumption-Family Questions

Assumption Question

A question that asks you to identify one of the unstated premises in an author's argument. Assumption questions come in two varieties.

Necessary Assumption questions ask you to identify an unstated premise required for an argument's conclusion to follow logically from its evidence. Typical question stems:

Which one of the following is an assumption on which the argument depends?

Which one of the following is an assumption that the argument requires in order for its conclusion to be properly drawn?

Sufficient Assumption questions ask you to identify an unstated premise sufficient to establish the argument's conclusion on the basis of its evidence. Typical question stems:

The conclusion follows logically if which one of the following is assumed?

Which one of the following, if assumed, enables the conclusion above to be properly inferred?

Strengthen/Weaken Question

A question that asks you to identify a fact that, if true, would make the argument's conclusion more likely (Strengthen) or less likely (Weaken) to follow from its evidence. Typical question stems:

Strengthen

Which one of the following, if true, most strengthens the argument above?

Which one the following, if true, most strongly supports the claim above?

Weaken

Which one of the following, if true, would most weaken the argument above?

Which one of the following, if true, most calls into question the claim above?

Flaw Question

A question that asks you to describe the reasoning error that the author has made in an argument. Typical question stems:

The argument's reasoning is most vulnerable to criticism on the grounds that the argument

Which of the following identifies a reasoning error in the argument?

The reasoning in the correspondent's argument is questionable because the argument

Parallel Flaw Question

A question that asks you to identify the argument that contains the same error(s) in reasoning that the argument in the stimulus contains. Typical question stems:

The pattern of flawed reasoning exhibited by the argument above is most similar to that exhibited in which one of the following?

Which one of the following most closely parallels the questionable reasoning cited above?

Evaluate the Argument Question

A question that asks you to identify an issue or consideration relevant to the validity of an argument. Think of Evaluate questions as "Strengthen or Weaken" questions. The correct answer, if true, will strengthen the argument, and if false, will weaken the argument, or vice versa. Evaluate questions are very rare. Typical question stems:

Which one of the following would be most useful to know in order to evaluate the legitimacy of the professor's argument?

It would be most important to determine which one of the following in evaluating the argument?

Non-Argument Questions

Inference Question

A question that asks you to identify a statement that follows from the statements in the stimulus. It is very important to note the characteristics of the one correct and the four incorrect answers before evaluating the choices in Inference questions. Depending on the wording of the question stem, the correct answer to an Inference question may be the one that

- *must be true* if the statements in the stimulus are true

- is *most strongly supported* by the statements in the stimulus

- *must be false* if the statements in the stimulus are true

Typical question stems:

If all of the statements above are true, then which one of the following must also be true?

Which one of the following can be properly inferred from the information above?

If the statements above are true, then each of the following could be true EXCEPT:

Which one of the following is most strongly supported by the information above?

The statements above, if true, most support which one of the following?

The facts described above provide the strongest evidence against which one of the following?

Paradox Question

A question that asks you to identify a fact that, if true, most helps to explain, resolve, or reconcile an apparent contradiction. Typical question stems:

Which one of the following, if true, most helps to explain how both studies' findings could be accurate?

Which one the following, if true, most helps to resolve the apparent conflict in the spokesperson's statements?

Each one of the following, if true, would contribute to an explanation of the apparent discrepancy in the information above EXCEPT:

Principle Questions

Principle Question

A question that asks you to identify corresponding cases and principles. Some Principle questions provide a principle in the stimulus and call for the answer choice describing a case that corresponds to the principle. Others provide a specific case in the stimulus and call for the answer containing a principle to which that case corresponds.

On the LSAT, Principle questions almost always mirror the skills rewarded by other Logical Reasoning question types. After each of the following Principle question stems, we note the question type it resembles. Typical question stems:

Which one of the following principles, if valid, most helps to justify the reasoning above? (**Strengthen**)

Which one of the following most accurately expresses the principle underlying the reasoning above? (**Assumption**)

The situation described above most closely conforms to which of the following generalizations? (**Inference**)

Which one of the following situations conforms most closely to the principle described above? (**Inference**)

Which one of the following principles, if valid, most helps to reconcile the apparent conflict among the prosecutor's claims? (**Paradox**)

Parallel Principle Question

A question that asks you to identify a specific case that illustrates the same principle that is illustrated by the case described in the stimulus. Typical question stem:

Of the following, which one illustrates a principle that is most similar to the principle illustrated by the passage?

Untangling the Stimulus

Conclusion Types

The conclusions in arguments found in the Logical Reasoning section of the LSAT tend to fall into one of six categories:

1) Value Judgment (an evaluative statement; e.g., Action X is unethical, or Y's recital was poorly sung)

2) "If"/Then (a conditional prediction, recommendation, or assertion; e.g., If X is true, then so is Y, or If you an M, then you should do N)

3) Prediction (X *will* or *will not* happen in the future)

4) Comparison (X is taller/shorter/more common/less common, etc. than Y)

5) Assertion of Fact (X is true or X is false)

6) Recommendation (we *should* or *should not* do X)

One-Sentence Test

A tactic used to identify the author's conclusion in an argument. Consider which sentence in the argument is the one the author would keep if asked to get rid of everything except her main point.

Subsidiary Conclusion

A conclusion following from one piece of evidence and then used by the author to support his overall conclusion or main point. Consider the following argument:

The pharmaceutical company's new experimental treatment did not succeed in clinical trials. As a result, the new treatment will not reach the market this year. Thus, the company will fall short of its revenue forecasts for the year.

Here, the sentence "As a result, the new treatment will not reach the market this year" is a subsidiary conclusion. It follows from the evidence that the new treatment failed in clinical trials, and it provides evidence for the overall conclusion that the company will not meet its revenue projections.

Keyword(s) in Logical Reasoning

A word or phrase that helps you untangle a question's stimulus by indicating the logical structure of the argument or the author's point. Here are three categories of Keywords to which LSAT experts pay special attention in Logical Reasoning:

Conclusion words; e.g., *therefore, thus, so, as a result, it follows that, consequently*, [evidence] *is evidence that* [conclusion]

Evidence word; e.g, *because, since, after all, for,* [evidence] *is evidence that* [conclusion]

Contrast words; e.g., *but, however, while, despite, in spite of, on the other hand* (These are especially useful in Paradox and Inference questions.)

Experts use Keywords even more extensively in Reading Comprehension. Learn the Keywords associated with the Reading Comprehension section, and apply them to Logical Reasoning when they are helpful.

Mismatched Concepts

One of two patterns to which authors' assumptions conform in LSAT arguments. Mismatched Concepts describes the assumption in arguments in which terms or concepts in the conclusion are different *in kind* from those in the evidence. The author assumes that there is a logical relationship between the different terms. For example:

Bobby is a **championship swimmer**. Therefore, he **trains every day**.

Here, the words "trains every day" appear only in the conclusion, and the words "championship swimmer" appear only in the evidence. For the author to reach this conclusion from this evidence, he assumes that championship swimmers train every day.

Another example:

Susan does **not eat her vegetables**. Thus, she will **not grow big and strong**.

In this argument, not growing big and strong is found only in the conclusion while not eating vegetables is found only in the evidence. For the author to reach this conclusion from this evidence, she must assume that eating one's vegetables is necessary for one to grow big and strong.

See also Overlooked Possibilities.

Overlooked Possibilities

One of two patterns to which authors' assumptions conform in LSAT arguments. Mismatched Concepts describes the assumption in arguments in which terms or concepts in the conclusion are different *in degree, scale, or level of certainty* from those in the evidence. The author assumes that there is no factor or explanation for the conclusion other than the one(s) offered in the evidence. For example:

Samson does not have a ticket stub for this movie showing. Thus, Samson must have sneaked into the movie without paying.

The author assumes that there is no other explanation for Samson's lack of a ticket stub. The author overlooks several possibilities: e.g., Samson had a special pass for this showing of the movie; Samson dropped his ticket stub by accident or threw it away after entering the theater; someone else in Samson's party has all of the party members' ticket stubs in her pocket or handbag.

Another example:

> Jonah's marketing plan will save the company money. Therefore, the company should adopt Jonah's plan.

Here, the author makes a recommendation based on one advantage. The author assumes that the advantage is the company's only concern or that there are no disadvantages that could outweigh it, e.g., Jonah's plan might save money on marketing but not generate any new leads or customers; Jonah's plan might damage the company's image or reputation; Jonah's plan might include illegal false advertising. Whenever the author of an LSAT argument concludes with a recommendation or a prediction based on just a single fact in the evidence, that author is always overlooking many other possibilities.

See also Mismatched Concepts.

Causal Argument

An argument in which the author concludes or assumes that one thing causes another. The most common pattern on the LSAT is for the author to conclude that A causes B from evidence that A and B are correlated. For example:

> I notice that whenever the store has a poor sales month, employee tardiness is also higher that month. Therefore, it must be that employee tardiness causes the store to lose sales.

The author assumes that the correlation in the evidence indicates a causal relationship. These arguments are vulnerable to three types of overlooked possibilities:

1) There could be **another causal factor**. In the previous example, maybe the months in question are those in which the manager takes vacation, causing the store to lose sales and permitting employees to arrive late without fear of the boss's reprimands.

2) Causation could be **reversed**. Maybe in months when sales are down, employee morale suffers and tardiness increases as a result.

3) The correlation could be **coincidental**. Maybe the correlation between tardiness and the dip in sales is pure coincidence.

See also Flaw Types: Correlation versus Causation.

Another pattern in causal arguments (less frequent on the LSAT) involves the assumption that a particular causal mechanism is or is not involved in a causal relationship. For example:

> The airport has rerouted takeoffs and landings so that they will not create noise over the Sunnyside neighborhood. Thus, the recent drop in Sunnyside's property values cannot be explained by the neighborhood's proximity to the airport.

Here, the author assumes that the only way that the airport could be the cause of dropping property values is through noise pollution. The author overlooks any other possible mechanism (e.g., frequent traffic jams and congestion) through which proximity to the airport could be cause of Sunnyside's woes.

Principle

A broad, law-like rule, definition, or generalization that covers a variety of specific cases with defined attributes. To see how principles are treated on the LSAT, consider the following principle:

> It is immoral for a person for his own gain to mislead another person.

That principle would cover a specific case, such as a seller who lies about the quality of construction to get a higher price for his house. It would also correspond to the case of a teenager who, wishing to spend a night out on the town, tells his mom "I'm going over to Randy's house." He knows that his mom believes that he will be staying at Randy's house, when in fact, he and Randy will go out together.

That principle does not, however, cover cases in which someone lies solely for the purpose of making the other person feel better or in which one person inadvertently misleads the other through a mistake of fact.

Be careful not to apply your personal ethics or morals when analyzing the principles articulated on the test.

Flaw Types

Necessary versus Sufficient

This flaw occurs when a speaker or author concludes that one event is necessary for a second event from evidence that the first event is sufficient to bring about the second event, or vice versa. Example:

> If more than 25,000 users attempt to access the new app at the same time, the server will crash. Last night, at 11:15 pm, the server crashed, so it must be case that more than 25,000 users were attempting to use the new app at that time.

In making this argument, the author assumes that the only thing that will cause the server to crash is the usage level (i.e., high usage is *necessary* for the server to crash). The evidence, however, says that high usage is one thing that will cause the server to crash (i.e., that high usage is *sufficient* to crash the server).

Correlation versus Causation

This flaw occurs when a speaker or author draws a conclusion that one thing causes another from evidence that the two things are correlated. Example:

Over the past half century, global sugar consumption has tripled. That same time period has seen a surge in the rate of technological advancement worldwide. It follows that the increase in sugar consumption has caused the acceleration in technological advancement.

In any argument with this structure, the author is making three unwarranted assumptions. First, he assumes that there is no alternate cause, i.e., there is nothing else that has contributed to rapid technological advancement. Second, he assumes that the causation is not reversed, i.e., technological advancement has not contributed to the increase in sugar consumption, perhaps by making it easier to grow, refine, or transport sugar. And, third, he assumes that the two phenomena are not merely coincidental, i.e., that it is not just happenstance that global sugar consumption is up at the same time that the pace of technological advancement has accelerated.

Unrepresentative Sample

This flaw occurs when a speaker or author draws a conclusion about a group from evidence in which the sample cannot represent that group because the sample is too small or too selective, or is biased in some way. Example:

> Moviegoers in our town prefer action films and romantic comedies over other film genres. Last Friday, we sent reporters to survey moviegoers at several theaters in town, and nearly 90 percent of those surveyed were going to watch either an action film or a romantic comedy.

The author assumes that the survey was representative of the town's moviegoers, but there are several reasons to question that assumption. First, we don't know how many people were actually surveyed. Even if the number of people surveyed was adequate, we don't know how many other types of movies were playing. Finally, the author doesn't limit her conclusion to moviegoers on Friday nights. If the survey had been conducted at Sunday matinees, maybe most moviegoers would have been heading out to see an animated family film or a historical drama. Who knows?

Scope Shift/Unwarranted Assumption

This flaw occurs when a speaker's or author's evidence has a scope or has terms different enough from the scope or terms in his conclusion that it is doubtful that the evidence can support the conclusion. Example:

> A very small percentage of working adults in this country can correctly define collateralized debt obligation securities. Thus, sad to say, the majority of the nation's working adults cannot make prudent choices about how to invest their savings.

This speaker assumes that prudent investing requires the ability to accurately define a somewhat obscure financial term. But prudence is not the same thing as expertise, and

the speaker does not offer any evidence that this knowledge of this particular term is related to wise investing.

Percent versus Number/Rate versus Number

This flaw occurs when a speaker or author draws a conclusion about real quantities from evidence about rates or percentages, or vice versa. Example:

> At the end of last season, Camp SunnyDay laid off half of their senior counselors and a quarter of their junior counselors. Thus, Camp SunnyDay must have more senior counselors than junior counselors.

The problem, of course, is that we don't know how many senior and junior counselors were on staff before the layoffs. If there were a total of 4 senior counselors and 20 junior counselors, then the camp would have laid off only 2 senior counselors while dismissing 5 junior counselors.

Equivocation

This flaw occurs when a speaker or author uses the same word in two different and incompatible ways. Example:

> Our opponent in the race has accused our candidate's staff members of behaving unprofessionally. But that's not fair. Our staff is made up entirely of volunteers, not paid campaign workers.

The speaker interprets the opponent's use of the word *professional* to mean "paid," but the opponent likely meant something more along the lines of "mature, competent, and businesslike."

Ad Hominem

This flaw occurs when a speaker or author concludes that another person's claim or argument is invalid because that other person has a personal flaw or shortcoming. One common pattern is for the speaker or author to claim the other person acts hypocritically or that the other person's claim is made from self-interest. Example:

> Mrs. Smithers testified before the city council, stating that the speed limits on the residential streets near her home are dangerously high. But why should we give her claim any credence? The way she eats and exercises, she's not even looking out for her own health.

The author attempts to undermine Mrs. Smithers's testimony by attacking her character and habits. He doesn't offer any evidence that is relevant to her claim about speed limits.

Part versus Whole

This flaw occurs when a speaker or author concludes that a part or individual has a certain characteristic because the whole or the larger group has that characteristic, or vice versa. Example:

> Patient: I should have no problems taking the three drugs prescribed to me by my doctors. I looked them up, and

none of the three is listed as having any major side effects.

Here, the patient is assuming that what is true of each of the drugs individually will be true of them when taken together. The patient's flaw is overlooking possible interactions that could cause problems not present when the drugs are taken separately.

Circular Reasoning

This flaw occurs when a speaker or author tries to prove a conclusion with evidence that is logically equivalent to the conclusion. Example:

> All those who run for office are prevaricators. To   see this, just consider politicians: they all prevaricate.

Perhaps the author has tried to disguise the circular reasoning in this argument by exchanging the words "those who run for office" in the conclusion for "politicians" in the evidence, but all this argument amounts to is "Politicians prevaricate; therefore, politicians prevaricate." On the LSAT, circular reasoning is very rarely the correct answer to a Flaw question, although it is regularly described in one of the wrong answers.

Question Strategies

Denial Test

A tactic for identifying the assumption *necessary* to an argument. When you negate an assumption necessary to an argument, the argument will fall apart. Negating an assumption that is not necessary to the argument will not invalidate the argument. Consider the following argument:

> Only high schools which produced a state champion athlete during the school year will be represented at the Governor's awards banquet. Therefore, McMurtry High School will be represented at the Governor's awards banquet.

Which one of the following is an assumption necessary to that argument?

(1) McMurtry High School produced more state champion athletes than any other high school during the school year.

(2) McMurtry High School produced at least one state champion athlete during the school year.

If you are at all confused about which of those two statements reflects the *necessary* assumption, negate them both.

(1) McMurtry High School **did not produce more** state champion athletes than any other high school during the school year.

That does not invalidate the argument. McMurtry could still be represented at the Governor's banquet.

(2) McMurtry High School **did not produce any** state champion athletes during the school year.

Here, negating the statement causes the argument to fall apart. Statement (2) is an assumption *necessary* to the argument.

Point at Issue "Decision Tree"

A tactic for evaluating the answer choices in Point at Issue questions. The correct answer is the only answer choice to which you can answer "Yes" to all three questions in the following diagram.

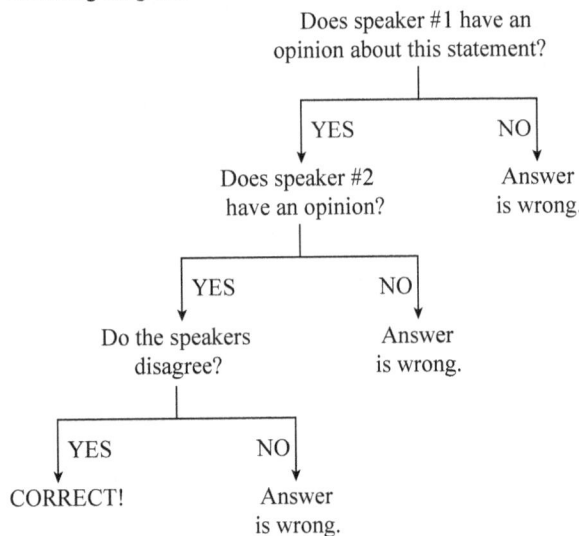

Common Methods of Argument

These methods of argument or argumentative strategies are common on the LSAT:

- Analogy, in which an author draws parallels between two unrelated (but purportedly similar) situations
- Example, in which an author cites a specific case or cases to justify a generalization
- Counterexample, in which an author seeks to discredit an opponent's argument by citing a specific case or cases that appear to invalidate the opponent's generalization
- Appeal to authority, in which an author cites an expert's claim or opinion as support for her conclusion
- Ad hominem attack, in which an author attacks her opponent's personal credibility rather than attacking the substance of her opponent's argument
- Elimination of alternatives, in which an author lists possibilities and discredits or rules out all but one

- Means/requirements, in which the author argues that something is needed to achieve a desired result

Wrong Answer Types in LR

Outside the Scope (Out of Scope; Beyond the Scope)

An answer choice containing a statement that is too broad, too narrow, or beyond the purview of the stimulus, making the statement in the choice irrelevant

180

An answer choice that directly contradicts what the correct answer must say (for example, a choice that strengthens the argument in a Weaken question)

Extreme

An answer choice containing language too emphatic to be supported by the stimulus; often (although not always) characterized by words such as *all, never, every, only,* or *most*

Distortion

An answer choice that mentions details from the stimulus but mangles or misstates what the author said about those details

Irrelevant Comparison

An answer choice that compares two items or attributes in a way not germane to the author's argument or statements

Half-Right/Half-Wrong

An answer choice that begins correctly, but then contradicts or distorts the passage in its second part; this wrong answer type is more common in Reading Comprehension than it is in Logical Reasoning

Faulty Use of Detail

An answer choice that accurately states something from the stimulus, but does so in a manner that answers the question incorrectly; this wrong answer type is more common in Reading Comprehension than it is in Logical Reasoning

Logic Games

Game Types

Strict Sequencing Game

A game that asks you to arrange entities into numbered positions or into a set schedule (usually hours or days). Strict Sequencing is, by far, the most common game type on the LSAT. In the typical Strict Sequencing game, there is a one-to-one matchup of entities and positions, e.g., seven entities to be placed in seven positions, one per position, or six entities to be placed over six consecutive days, one entity per day.

From time to time, the LSAT will offer Strict Sequencing with more entities than positions (e.g., seven entities to be arranged over five days, with some days to receive more than one entity) or more positions than entities (e.g., six entities to be scheduled over seven days, with at least one day to receive no entities).

Other, less common variations on Strict Sequencing include:

Double Sequencing, in which each entity is placed or scheduled two times (there have been rare occurrences of Triple or Quadruple Sequencing). Alternatively, a Double Sequencing game may involve two different sets of entities each sequenced once.

Circular Sequencing, in which entities are arranged around a table or in a circular arrangement (NOTE: When the positions in a Circular Sequencing game are numbered, the first and last positions are adjacent.)

Vertical Sequencing, in which the positions are numbered from top to bottom or from bottom to top (as in the floors of a building)

Loose Sequencing Game

A game that asks you to arrange or schedule entities in order but provides no numbering or naming of the positions. The rules in Loose Sequencing give only the relative positions (earlier or later, higher or lower) between two entities or among three entities. Loose Sequencing games almost always provide that there will be no ties between entities in the rank, order, or position they take.

Circular Sequencing Game

See Strict Sequencing Game.

Selection Game

A game that asks you to choose or include some entities from the initial list of entities and to reject or exclude others. Some Selection games provide overall limitations on the number of entities to be selected (e.g., "choose exactly four of seven students" or "choose at least two of six entrees") while others provide little or no restriction on the number selected ("choose at least one type of flower" or "select from among seven board members").

Distribution Game

A game that asks you to break up the initial list of entities into two, three, or (very rarely) four groups or teams. In the vast majority of Distribution games, each entity is assigned to one and only one group or team. A relatively common variation on Distribution games will provide a subdivided list of entities (e.g., eight students—four men and four women—will form three study groups) and will then require representatives from those subdivisions on each team (e.g., each study group will have at least one of the men on it).

Matching Game

A game that asks you to match one or more members of one set of entities to specific members of another set of entities, or that asks you to match attributes or objects to a set of entities. Unlike Distribution games, in which each entity is placed in exactly one group or team, Matching games usually permit you to assign the same attribute or object to more than one entity.

In some cases, there are overall limitations on the number of entities that can be matched (e.g., "In a school's wood shop, there are four workstations—numbered 1 through 4—and each workstation has at least one and at most three of the following tools—band saw, dremmel tool, electric sander, and power drill"). In almost all Matching games, further restrictions on the number of entities that can be matched to a particular person or place will be found in the rules (e.g., Workstation 4 will have more tools than Workstation 2 has).

Hybrid Game

A game that asks you to do two (or rarely, three) of the standard actions (Sequencing, Selection, Distribution, and Matching) to a set of entities.

The most common Hybrid is Sequencing-Matching. A typical Sequencing-Matching Hybrid game might ask you to schedule six speakers at a conference to six one-hour speaking slots (from 9 am to 2 pm), and then assign each speaker one of two subjects (economic development or trade policy).

Nearly as common as Sequencing-Matching is Distribution-Sequencing. A typical game of this type might ask you to divide six people in a talent competition into either a Dance category or a Singing category, and then rank the competitors in each category.

It is most common to see one Hybrid game in each Logic Games section, although there have been tests with two Hybrid games and tests with none. To determine the type of Hybrid you are faced with, identify the game's action in Step 1 of the Logic Games Method. For example, a game asking you to choose four of six runners, and then assign the four chosen runners to lanes numbered 1 through 4 on a track, would be a Selection-Sequencing Hybrid game.

Mapping Game

A game that provides you with a description of geographical locations and, typically, of the connections among them. Mapping games often ask you to determine the shortest possible routes between two locations or to account for the number of connections required to travel from one location to another. This game type is extremely rare, and as of February 2017, a Mapping game was last seen on PrepTest 40 administered in June 2003.

Process Game

A game that opens with an initial arrangement of entities (e.g., a starting sequence or grouping) and provides rules that describe the processes through which that arrangement can be altered. The questions typically ask you for acceptable arrangements or placements of particular entities after one, two, or three stages in the process. Occasionally, a Process game question might provide information about the arrangement after one, two, or three stages in the process and ask you what must have happened in the earlier stages. This game type is extremely rare, and as of November 2016, a Process game was last seen on PrepTest 16 administered in September 1995. However, there was a Process game on PrepTest 80, administered in December 2016, thus ending a 20-year hiatus.

Game Setups and Deductions

Floater

An entity that is not restricted by any rule or limitation in the game

Blocks of Entities

Two or more entities that are required by rule to be adjacent or separated by a set number of spaces (Sequencing games), to be placed together in the same group (Distribution games), to be matched to the same entity (Matching games), or to be selected or rejected together (Selection games)

Limited Options

Rules or restrictions that force all of a game's acceptable arrangements into two (or occasionally three) patterns

Established Entities

An entity required by rule to be placed in one space or assigned to one particular group throughout the entire game

Number Restrictions

Rules or limitations affecting the number of entities that may be placed into a group or space throughout the game

Duplications

Two or more rules that restrict a common entity. Usually, these rules can be combined to reach additional deductions. For example, if you know that B is placed earlier than A in a sequence and that C is placed earlier than B in that sequence, you can deduce that C is placed earlier than A in the sequence and that there is at least one space (the space occupied by B) between C and A.

Master Sketch

The final sketch derived from the game's setup, rules, and deductions. LSAT experts preserve the Master Sketch for reference as they work through the questions. The Master

Sketch does not include any conditions from New-"If" question stems.

Logic Games Question Types

Acceptability Question

A question in which the correct answer is an acceptable arrangement of all the entities relative to the spaces, groups, or selection criteria in the game. Answer these by using the rules to eliminate answer choices that violate the rules.

Partial Acceptability Question

A question in which the correct answer is an acceptable arrangement of some of the entities relative to some of the spaces, groups, or selection criteria in the game, and in which the arrangement of entities not included in the answer choices could be acceptable to the spaces, groups, or selection criteria not explicitly shown in the answer choices. Answer these the same way you would answer Acceptability questions, by using the rules to eliminate answer choices that explicitly or implicitly violate the rules.

Must Be True/False; Could Be True/False Question

A question in which the correct answer must be true, could be true, could be false, or must be false (depending on the question stem), and in which no additional rules or conditions are provided by the question stem

New-"If" Question

A question in which the stem provides an additional rule, condition, or restriction (applicable only to that question), and then asks what must/could be true/false as a result. LSAT experts typically handle New-"If" questions by copying the Master Sketch, adding the new restriction to the copy, and working out any additional deductions available as a result of the new restriction before evaluating the answer choices.

Rule Substitution Question

A question in which the correct answer is a rule that would have an impact identical to one of the game's original rules on the entities in the game

Rule Change Question

A question in which the stem alters one of the original rules in the game, and then asks what must/could be true/false as a result. LSAT experts typically handle Rule Change questions by reconstructing the game's sketch, but now accounting for the changed rule in place of the original. These questions are rare on recent tests.

Rule Suspension Question

A question in which the stem indicates that you should ignore one of the original rules in the game, and then asks what must/could be true/false as a result. LSAT experts typically handle Rule Suspension questions by reconstructing

the game's sketch, but now accounting for the absent rule. These questions are very rare.

Complete and Accurate List Question

A question in which the correct answer is a list of any and all entities that could acceptably appear in a particular space or group, or a list of any and all spaces or groups in which a particular entity could appear

Completely Determine Question

A question in which the correct answer is a condition that would result in exactly one acceptable arrangement for all of the entities in the game

Supply the "If" Question

A question in which the correct answer is a condition that would guarantee a particular result stipulated in the question stem

Minimum/Maximum Question

A question in which the correct answer is the number corresponding to the fewest or greatest number of entities that could be selected (Selection), placed into a particular group (Distribution), or matched to a particular entity (Matching). Often, Minimum/Maximum questions begin with New-"If" conditions.

Earliest/Latest Question

A question in which the correct answer is the earliest or latest position in which an entity may acceptably be placed. Often, Earliest/Latest questions begin with New-"If" conditions.

"How Many" Question

A question in which the correct answer is the exact number of entities that may acceptably be placed into a particular group or space. Often, "How Many" questions begin with New-"If" conditions.

Reading Comprehension
Strategic Reading

Roadmap

The test taker's markup of the passage text in Step 1 (Read the Passage Strategically) of the Reading Comprehension Method. To create helpful Roadmaps, LSAT experts circle or underline Keywords in the passage text and jot down brief, helpful notes or paragraph summaries in the margin of their test booklets.

Keyword(s) in Reading Comprehension

Words in the passage text that reveal the passage structure or the author's point of view and thus help test takers anticipate and research the questions that accompany the passage. LSAT experts pay attention to six categories of Keywords in Reading Comprehension:

Emphasis/Opinion—words that signal that the author finds a detail noteworthy or that the author has positive or negative opinion about a detail; any subjective or evaluative language on the author's part (e.g., *especially, crucial, unfortunately, disappointing, I suggest, it seems likely*)

Contrast—words indicating that the author finds two details or ideas incompatible or that the two details illustrate conflicting points (e.g., *but, yet, despite, on the other hand*)

Logic—words that indicate an argument, either the author's or someone else's (e.g., *thus, therefore, because, it follows that*)

Illustration—words indicating an example offered to clarify or support another point (e.g., *for example, this shows, to illustrate*)

Sequence/Chronology—words showing steps in a process or developments over time (e.g., *traditionally, in the past, today, first, second, finally, earlier, subsequent*)

Continuation—words indicating that a subsequent example or detail supports the same point or illustrates the same idea as the previous example (e.g., *moreover, in addition, also, further, along the same lines*)

Margin Notes

The brief notes or paragraph summaries that the test taker jots down next to the passage in the margin of the test booklet

Big Picture Summaries: Topic/Scope/Purpose/Main Idea

A test taker's mental summary of the passage as a whole made during Step 1 (Read the Passage Strategically) of the Reading Comprehension Method. LSAT experts account for four aspects of the passage in their big picture summaries:

Topic—the overall subject of the passage

Scope—the particular aspect of the Topic that the author focuses on

Purpose—the author's reason or motive for writing the passage (express this as a verb; e.g., *to refute, to outline, to evaluate, to critique*)

Main Idea—the author's conclusion or overall takeaway; if the passage does not contain an explicit conclusion or thesis, you can combine the author's Scope and Purpose to get a good sense of the Main Idea.

Passage Types

Kaplan categorizes Reading Comprehension passages in two ways, by subject matter and by passage structure.

Subject matter categories

In the majority of LSAT Reading Comprehension sections, there is one passage from each of the following subject matter categories:

Humanities—topics from art, music, literature, philosophy, etc.

Natural Science—topics from biology, astronomy, paleontology, physics, etc.

Social Science—topics from anthropology, history, sociology, psychology, etc.

Law—topics from constitutional law, international law, legal education, jurisprudence, etc.

Passage structure categories

The majority of LSAT Reading Comprehension passages correspond to one of the following descriptions. The first categories—Theory/Perspective and Event/Phenomenon—have been the most common on recent LSATs.

Theory/Perspective—The passage focuses on a thinker's theory or perspective on some aspect of the Topic; typically (though not always), the author disagrees and critiques the thinker's perspective and/or defends his own perspective.

Event/Phenomenon—The passage focuses on an event, a breakthrough development, or a problem that has recently arisen; when a solution to the problem is proposed, the author most often agrees with the solution (and that represents the passage's Main Idea).

Biography—The passage discusses something about a notable person; the aspect of the person's life emphasized by the author reflects the Scope of the passage.

Debate—The passage outlines two opposing positions (neither of which is the author's) on some aspect of the Topic; the author may side with one of the positions, may remain neutral, or may critique both. (This structure has been relatively rare on recent LSATs.)

Comparative Reading

A pair of passages (labeled Passage A and Passage B) that stand in place of the typical single passage exactly one time in each Reading Comprehension section administered since June 2007. The paired Comparative Reading passages share the same Topic, but may have different Scopes and Purposes. On most LSAT tests, a majority of the questions accompanying Comparative Reading passages require the test taker to compare or contrast ideas or details from both passages.

Question Strategies

Research Clues

A reference in a Reading Comprehension question stem to a word, phrase, or detail in the passage text, or to a particular line number or paragraph in the passage. LSAT experts recognize five kinds of research clues:

Line Reference—An LSAT expert researches around the referenced lines, looking for Keywords that indicate why the referenced details were included or how they were used by the author.

Paragraph Reference—An LSAT expert consults her passage Roadmap to see the paragraph's Scope and Purpose.

Quoted Text (often accompanied by a line reference)—An LSAT expert checks the context of the quoted term or phrase, asking what the author meant by it in the passage.

Proper Nouns—An LSAT expert checks the context of the person, place, or thing in the passage, asking whether the author made a positive, negative, or neutral evaluation of it and why the author included it in the passage.

Content Clues—These are terms, concepts, or ideas from the passage mentioned in the question stem but not as direct quotes and not accompanied by line references. An LSAT expert knows that content clues almost always refer to something that the author emphasized or about which the author expressed an opinion.

Reading Comp Question Types

Global Question

A question that asks for the Main Idea of the passage or for the author's primary Purpose in writing the passage. Typical question stems:

Which one of the following most accurately expresses the main point of the passage?

The primary purpose of the passage is to

Detail Question

A question that asks what the passage explicitly states about a detail. Typical question stems:

According to the passage, some critics have criticized Gilliam's films on the grounds that

The passage states that one role of a municipality's comptroller in budget decisions by the city council is to

The author identifies which one of the following as a commonly held but false preconception?

The passage contains sufficient information to answer which of the following questions?

Occasionally, the test will ask for a correct answer that contains a detail *not* stated in the passage:

The author attributes each of the following positions to the Federalists EXCEPT:

Inference Question

A question that asks for a statement that follows from or is based on the passage but that is not necessarily stated explicitly in the passage. Some Inference questions contain research clues. The following are typical Inference question stems containing research clues:

Based on the passage, the author would be most likely to agree with which one of the following statements about unified field theory?

The passage suggests which one of the following about the behavior of migratory water fowl?

Given the information in the passage, to which one of the following would radiocarbon dating techniques likely be applicable?

Other Inference questions lack research clues in the question stem. They may be evaluated using the test taker's Big Picture Summaries, or the answer choices may make it clear that the test taker should research a particular part of the passage text. The following are typical Inference question stems containing research clues:

It can be inferred from the passage that the author would be most likely to agree that

Which one of the following statements is most strongly supported by the passage?

Other Reading Comprehension question types categorized as Inference questions are Author's Attitude questions and Vocabulary-in-Context questions.

Logic Function Question

A question that asks why the author included a particular detail or reference in the passage or how the author used a particular detail or reference. Typical question stems:

The author of the passage mentions declining inner-city populations in the paragraph most likely in order to

The author's discussion of Rimbaud's travels in the Mediterranean (lines 23–28) functions primarily to

Which one of the following best expresses the function of the third paragraph in the passage?

Logic Reasoning Question

A question that asks the test taker to apply Logical Reasoning skills in relation to a Reading Comprehension passage. Logic Reasoning questions often mirror Strengthen or Parallel Reasoning questions, and occasionally mirror Method of Argument or Principle questions. Typical question stems:

Which one of the following, if true, would most strengthen the claim made by the author in the last sentence of the passage (lines 51–55)?

Which one of the following pairs of proposals is most closely analogous to the pair of studies discussed in the passage?

Author's Attitude Question

A question that asks for the author's opinion or point of view on the subject discussed in the passage or on a detail mentioned in the passage. Since the correct answer may follow from the passage without being explicitly stated in it, some Author's Attitude questions are characterized as a subset of Inference questions. Typical question stems:

> The author's attitude toward the use of DNA evidence in the appeals by convicted felons is most accurately described as

> The author's stance regarding monetarist economic theories can most accurately be described as one of

Vocabulary-in-Context Question

A question that asks how the author uses a word or phrase within the context of the passage. The word or phrase in question is always one with multiple meanings. Since the correct answer follows from its use in the passage, Vocabulary-in-Context questions are characterized as a subset of Inference questions. Typical question stems:

> Which one of the following is closest in meaning to the word "citation" as it used in the second paragraph of the passage (line 18)?

> In context, the word "enlightenment" (line 24) refers to

Wrong Answer Types in RC

Outside the Scope (Out of Scope; Beyond the Scope)

An answer choice containing a statement that is too broad, too narrow, or beyond the purview of the passage

180

An answer choice that directly contradicts what the correct answer must say

Extreme

An answer choice containing language too emphatic (e.g., *all*, *never*, *every*, *none*) to be supported by the passage

Distortion

An answer choice that mentions details or ideas from the passage but mangles or misstates what the author said about those details or ideas

Faulty Use of Detail

An answer choice that accurately states something from the passage but in a manner that incorrectly answers the question

Half-Right/Half-Wrong

An answer choice in which one clause follows from the passage while another clause contradicts or deviates from the passage

Formal Logic Terms

Conditional Statement ("If"-Then Statement)

A statement containing a sufficient clause and a necessary clause. Conditional statements can be described in Formal Logic shorthand as:

> If [sufficient clause]   → [necessary clause]

In some explanations, the LSAT expert may refer to the sufficient clause as the statement's "trigger" and to the necessary clause as the statement's result.

For more on how to interpret, describe, and use conditional statements on the LSAT, please refer to "A Note About Formal Logic on the LSAT" in this book's introduction.

Contrapositive

The conditional statement logically equivalent to another conditional statement formed by reversing the order of and negating the terms in the original conditional statement. For example, reversing and negating the terms in this statement:

> If   A   →   B

results in its contrapositive:

> If   ~B   →   ~A

To form the contrapositive of conditional statements in which either the sufficient clause or the necessary clause has more than one term, you must also change the conjunction *and* to *or*, or vice versa. For example, reversing and negating the terms and changing *and* to *or* in this statement:

> If   M   →   O AND P

results in its contrapositive:

> If   ~O OR ~P   →   ~M

www.ingramcontent.com/pod-product-compliance
Lightning Source LLC
Chambersburg PA
CBHW081259040426
42452CB00014B/2573